John Carroll

# Agile Project Management

In easy steps is an imprint of In Easy Steps Limited
4 Chapel Court · 42 Holly Walk · Leamington Spa
Warwickshire · United Kingdom · CV32 4YS
www.ineasysteps.com



In Easy Steps Limited supports The Forest Stewardship Council (FSC), the leading international forest certification organisation. All our titles that are printed on Greenpeace approved FSC certified paper carry the FSC logo.

MIX
Paper from responsible sources
FSC® C020837

Printed and bound in the United Kingdom

ISBN 978-1-84078-447-3

# Contents

# 1 Agile Projects

*This chapter provides the background to the need for an agile approach to projects. It covers the benefits of using an agile approach and the typical components of an agile project.*

# Introduction

This book is primarily intended for project managers who are moving into the project management of agile projects. It will also be of interest to agile developers who wish to know more about project management. And finally it will also be of interest to anyone else who wishes to know more about the management of agile projects.

**Beware**

This book is not a basic introduction to project management. That is covered in Effective Project Management in easy steps.

## Traditional Projects

The traditional approach to projects and project management started by defining exactly what the project was expected to produce. This was termed the requirements or specification and was agreed and signed off between the project team and the business or customer.

The project team then went away and built a product or system that they thought met those requirements and, some time later, presented the finished product to the customer. The problems with this approach are set out later in this chapter but the end result was all too often that it was not what the customer needed.

## Agile Projects

The agile approach to projects starts out with the expectation that the requirements (or features) will evolve and change during the course of the project. What is fixed and agreed between the project team and the customer is the resources that will be used and the time that will be taken by the project team to deliver as much as possible of the prioritized features the customer wants. The difference between the two approaches is illustrated below:

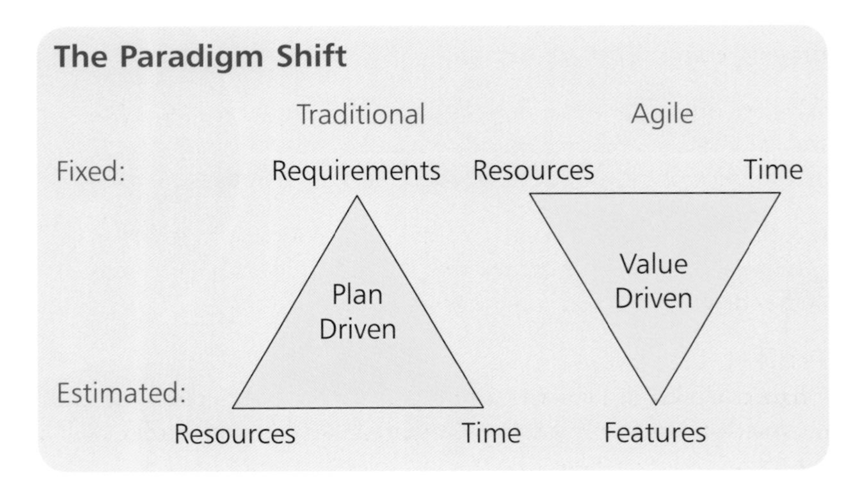

# About the Book

This first chapter provides an introduction to agile projects, beginning with some of the difficulties of using the traditional approach and how the agile approach deals with them. It then examines the typical components of an agile project.

## Agile Project Management

Chapter two goes through the details of agile project management starting with the differences between this and the traditional approach to project management. It then sets out a framework of agile project management, which covers all aspects of project managing an agile project.

## Other Agile Components

While there are a wide variety of methods and processes that could be defined as agile, the best defined and most typical components are covered in chapters three to six. These are the Dynamic Systems Development Method (DSDM), Scrum, Extreme Programming and Lean Development.

## Getting Started

Chapter seven deals with the agile approach to starting up a project including pre-project activities and establishing the feasibility. It covers producing the terms of reference, feasibility assessment and the outline project plan.

## Project Phases

The next three chapters cover the main project phases of an agile project. Chapter eight introduces the foundation phase, including establishing the business foundations, developing the requirements list, systems architecture, development approach, solution prototype and delivery plan.

Chapter nine covers the development of the solution including the exploration and engineering phases. It also covers product assurance, testing, deployment planning and review.

Chapter ten covers the deployment of the solution together with the project and increment reviews. It looks at benefits enablement and ends with the end project assessment.

## Project Closure

Chapter eleven deals with closing the project down, planning and conducting a post-project benefits assessments. It concludes with a set of guiding principles for the success of an agile project.

# The Problems

Traditional project methodology originally evolved from the construction industry, where the prohibitive cost of making late changes meant requirements were frozen as early as possible. It was based on a sequential design process often referred to as the waterfall model, so called as progress is seen as flowing steadily downwards (like a waterfall) through the stages of the project, each stage building on the work of the preceding stage.

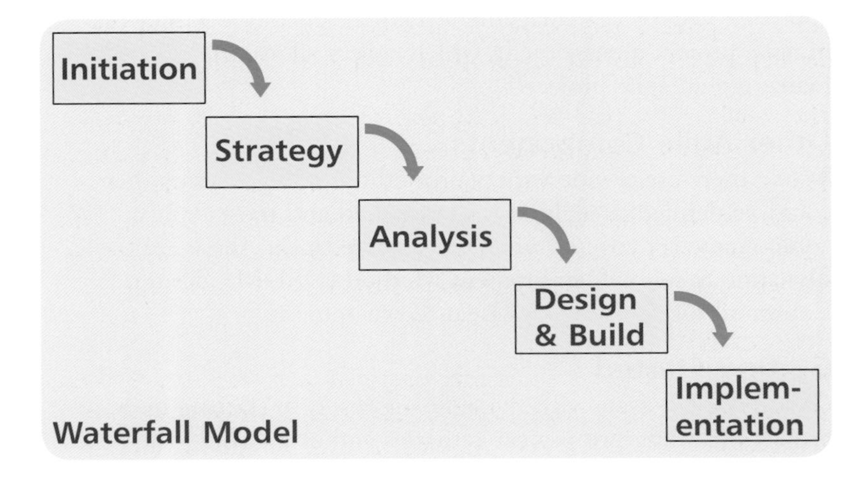


## Fixed Requirements

This methodology was initially adopted by software developers but it did not always suit the software development process, where requirements could (and very often did) change through the course of a project. Various attempts were made to deal with this, such as 'upstream propagation' in which changes made later in the project were fed back upstream to the earlier stages of the project and the requirements were then changed.

While this had some success a more radical alternative was needed and methodologies such as Rapid Application Development (RAD), Spiral, Iterative and Incremental were developed. In these the requirements are developed throughout the life of the project and delivered through a series of releases, which gradually deliver more functionality to the customer.

In addition to the rigid methodology and project life-cycle being used there were a couple of further problems stemming from the use of the traditional approach.

## Business Involvement

In the traditional approach the business was kept well away from the development team. They were consulted in the early stages to define the requirements and they were involved at the end to test the finished product. But if they saw what was being done during the project, they might well decide it was wrong and ask the developers to change it. This would be disastrous for the project as re-working and the consequent need for re-testing would delay the project. Delivering on time was the prime aim of the developers, although it was rarely achieved.

The problem was that delivering something on time that was not what the business needed was an even worse outcome. It gradually dawned on people that it was better to involve the business actively in the project. By having them involved right through the project it would at least ensure that what was delivered was what the business needed, even if it was a little late.

## Project Management

Traditionally the project manager operated in what has now been referred to as a Command and Control style. In this the project manager developed the detailed project plan, identifying all the tasks that required completion. They then allocated tasks to each member of the project team telling them exactly what to do. While this might, originally, have been fine for the construction industry it did not get the best or most creative output from software or engineering developers.

The solution was to empower the project team more and actively engage them in developing the detailed plans for the project. That way the plans were not only likely to be better but the developers would also be more committed to them. Secondly, by allowing the developers to decide for themselves what needed to be done to deliver the requirements, they could make best use of the skills and knowledge of each team member and probably get much better commitment from the team members.

These types of changes to the methods being used on software development projects began to be referred to as lightweight methods to differentiate them from the old heavyweight approach. These included DSDM, Scrum, Extreme Programming, Lean Development, Agile Testing and several more.

# The Agile Manifesto

In February 2001, representatives and users of most of the more popular lightweight development methods met at the Snowbird ski resort in Utah to discuss the need for an alternative to the existing heavyweight, documentation-dependent, software development processes. At the end of the conference, they published their manifesto to define the approach now known as agile development. The manifesto reads as follows:

**The Agile Manifesto**

We are uncovering better ways of developing software by doing it and helping others do it. Through this work we have come to value:

*Individuals and interactions* over *processes and tools*

*Working software* over *comprehensive documentation*

*Customer collaboration* over *contract negotiation*

*Responding to change* over *following a plan*

That is, while there is value in the items on the right, we value the items on the left more.

## What it Means

The meanings of the manifesto items on the left within the agile software development context are as described below:

- Individuals and Interactions: in an agile development, self-organization and motivation are important, as are interactions like co-location and pair programming
- Working Software: working software will be much more useful and welcome than just presenting detailed documents to clients in meetings
- Customer Collaboration: requirements cannot be fully defined at the beginning of the software development cycle, therefore continuous customer involvement is very important
- Responding to Change: agile development is focused on quick responses to change and continuous development, harnessing change for the customer's competitive advantage

## Twelve Principles

These twelve principles underlie this agile manifesto:

1. Customer Satisfaction: by the early and the continuing delivery of useful software
2. Changing Requirements: welcome changing requirements, even late in the development process
3. Frequent Delivery: of working software, from every couple of weeks to every couple of months
4. Measure of Progress: delivery of working software is the principle measurement of progress
5. Sustainable Development: so the sponsors, developers and users can maintain a constant pace indefinitely
6. Close Cooperation: business people and developers must work together daily throughout the project
7. Motivated Individuals: by giving them the support they need and trusting them to get the job done
8. Face-to-face Conversation: the most efficient and effective method of conveying information in a development team
9. Technical Excellence: through continuous attention to technical excellence and good design
10. Simplicity: by keeping things simple the amount of work that has to be done is minimized
11. Self-organizing teams: the best architectures, requirements and designs emerge from self-organizing teams
12. Regular Adaptation: the team reflects on how to become more effective and adjusts its behavior accordingly

# Agile Approach

As we have already seen, traditionally project management and software development were largely based on a sequential design process referred to as the 'waterfall' model. However this did not suit the software development process, where requirements could and often did change during the course of a project and more agile methods were evolved.

## Project Management Methodology

Although traditional project management methodology can be applied to all types of projects there are some special constraints that apply to agile projects. The features (requirements) are allowed to change and evolve through the life of the project, while the resources and time are frozen. So the project will deliver as much of the prioritized requirements as can be delivered in the available time and within the cost budget.

Within each phase of an agile project, the developers collaborate closely with representatives of the business or customer so they understand the detail of the next step and can create an evolving solution. Before the product, process or software goes into production the business can decide if they want to continue on the same path or make alterations.

## Agile Project Management

Because of the radical nature of these methods, the traditional (waterfall based) approach to project management, with requirements being defined and fixed early in the project, did not fit comfortably with this new approach. So a new form of agile project management began to develop.

In 2010 the DSDM Consortium published a definition of Agile Project Management, based on the DSDM method and interfacing with other agile methods such as Scrum and XP. This Agile Project Management differs from traditional project management in a number of key respects:

## Management Style

On a traditional project, the project manager may be actively involved in directing the work of the team and telling them what to do. This is sometimes referred to as Command and Control. In agile project management the project manager is more of a facilitator and their role is to ensure that the collaboration between the business and the developers is effective.

### Features

As the required features are expected to develop and change during the project the traditional approach of fixing requirements and allowing time and resources to flex to meet them is reversed. In an agile project time and resources are fixed (through time-boxing) and features are allowed to change at the start of each new iteration of the product.

### Planning

In a traditional project the project manager would develop and own the project plan. In an agile project the features are constantly changing, so planning for each phase, release or iteration is carried out as late as possible. Further, although the outline project plan is produced by the project manager, the detailed plans are produced by the development team.

### Project Phases

In place of the traditional (waterfall) project stages, agile projects use a number of phases, containing several iterations, leading to a number of product releases and therefore a series of implementations.

### Change Control

The traditional project concept of change control is replaced by the features backlog. This is a list of prioritized business requirements, which is controlled by the business.

### Risk Management

In place of the traditional approach to risk management and concerns about scope creep a broader approach to risk is taken in an agile project. The developers own the development risks and the business takes a more proactive role as the product owner.

### Organization

In a traditional project the project manager hands out work packets to the team. In an agile project this is managed by the development team and the project manager takes on more of a supportive role to the team.

### Monitoring Progress

In a traditional project the project manager has a detailed Gantt chart against which to monitor progress. In an agile project their role is to record the effort used on a burndown chart.

**Hot tip**

In an agile project, the project manager's role is to facilitate and support the team, not to tell them what to do.

# The Benefits

The traditional (or waterfall) project management methodology, has been criticized for not being able to cope with constant changes in software or other types of development projects. This is probably the single most significant benefit of using agile methodology.

## Changing Requirements

Not only does the agile approach have the benefit of dealing with changing requirements, it also overcomes the difficulty that customers have in adequately specifying their requirements in the first place, before they have even seen some sort of prototype. Specifying requirements before starting the actual development places a huge and unnecessary overhead on the project and is likely to cause long delays to the project starting to produce anything. The iterative nature of the agile approach makes it an excellent choice when it comes to managing development projects.

## Customer Involvement

Failure to involve the business or external customer fully in the project is likely to lead to their eventual dissatisfaction with the final product. Close involvement of the customer means they can share the decision making, set the priorities and agree on the best solution to any issues. They will be committed to the final product and it will meet their requirements.

## Quick Results

The use of agile methods ensures that the project delivers a quality product much earlier than would happen on a traditional project. The product will not yet have all of the required features but, on the Pareto principle, the delivery of the most important 20% of the features is likely to deliver around 80% of the benefits.

## Progress Measurement

Using the delivery of a series of working products as the main form of progress measurement is one that everyone involved in the project can understand. The project manager can measure and report on it. The developers can work to delivering it and the customers can touch and feel it.

## Team Motivation

By empowering the development team, allowing them to organize themselves and having active customer involvement the team will be much more highly motivated and produce better results. Close cooperation on a daily basis with the customer will also add to their motivation and the delivery of a better product.

## Product Quality

The focus on technical excellence and good design in an agile project coupled with continuous testing will ensure that a product of excellent quality is delivered. The close involvement of the customer will ensure their feedback to the process so that the product is not only excellent but it is what the customer needs.

## The Ideal Project

We can now begin to see the type of project that can most benefit from the use of agile methods. Any development type project that has poorly defined requirements will benefit from the agile approach. The project should also have a fairly short timeline, ideally less than one year. The business or customer has to be able to make use of iterative product delivery with gradually enhanced features. The development team should not be too large because of the close cooperation and face-to-face working methods. A large team would begin to place a heavy communications burden on the project.

Hot tip

If your project fits this profile you should seriously consider using agile methodology.

## Disadvantages

Having established the ideal type of project to benefit from the agile approach, we can now see where it would not be beneficial. If this were not the case then all projects would be run using agile methods.

Many project management practitioners believe that agile methods do not scale well. Hence large-scale projects (even software development projects) should probably still be conducted using the traditional waterfall development and project management methods.

The strength and usefulness of agile methods are both clearly demonstrated in projects with poorly-defined and frequently changing requirements. So it would not seem to offer any advantage over traditional methodology when it comes to projects where the requirements are clearly defined and unlikely to change significantly over the course of the project. So large projects with clear requirements (such as major construction projects) are probably best managed using the traditional methods.

Beware

If your project fits this profile you should not be considering the use of agile methodology.

# Project Components

In addition to Agile Project Management, the other typical agile methods that may be used on an agile project include: DSDM, Scrum, Extreme Programming and Lean Software Development. The relationship between these elements is illustrated in the following method coverage diagram:

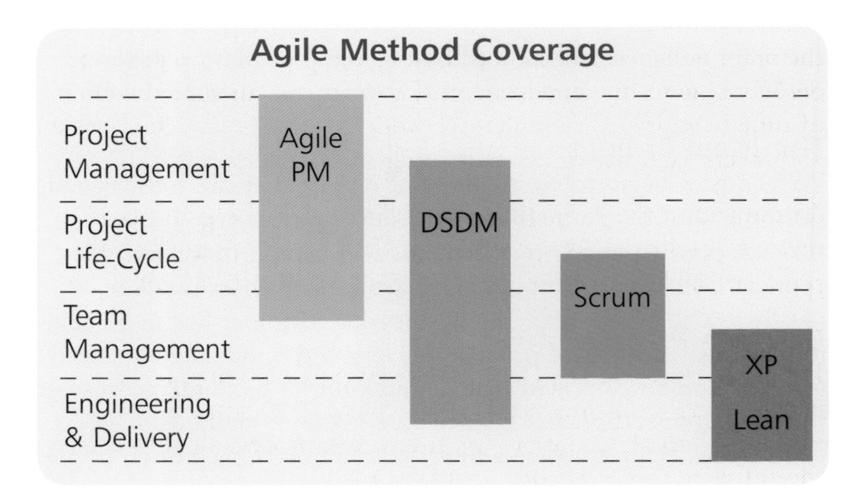


As can be seen from the diagram above, there is a significant amount of coverage cross-over between the various methods. All of these agile methods are compatible and to a certain extent complimentary. Where the methods are not fully complimentary, then the most suitable method for the particular project can be selected by the project team.

## Project Management

Agile Project Management was a new initiative launched in 2010 by the DSDM Consortium (www.dsdm.org) . It took the project management and project life-cycle elements of DSDM and enhanced them by the addition of advice and guidance based on existing good practice. This methodology enables project managers to adopt an agile approach within their organizations and to interface well with agile development teams.

## DSDM

The Dynamic Systems Development Model provides a framework for agile project delivery, which provides best practice guidance for the delivery of quality products on time and within budget. It is designed to be tailored and used in conjunction with other agile methodology and traditional configuration and quality management systems.

## Scrum

Scrum was originally formalized for software development projects, but works well for any complex, innovative project. Starting with the prioritized product backlog (requirements), the team pulls a small number from the top of that backlog and decides how to implement them. The team has an agreed amount of time (a sprint) to complete its work (usually two to four weeks) and meets each day to assess its progress (daily scrum).

At the end of the sprint, the work is delivered, the sprint is reviewed and the next sprint begins. This continues until all the product backlog has been completed or the time box ends.

## Extreme Programming

Extreme Programming (XP) is another popular agile process, which stresses customer satisfaction. Instead of delivering everything on some date in the future this process aims to deliver the software that is needed as it is needed.

Extreme Programming allows the software developers to respond confidently to changing customer requirements, even late in the life cycle. Extreme Programming emphasizes teamwork with management, customers and developers all being equal partners in a collaborative team. The team is self-organized around the problem to solve it as efficiently as possible.

## Lean Development

Lean Software Development was developed from the manufacturing process of the same name and follows agile principles. Lean development can be summarized by seven major principles which are again based on lean manufacturing principles: Eliminate Waste (including unnecessary code and functionality); Amplify Learning; Decide as Late as Possible; Deliver as Fast as Possible; Empower the Team; Build Integrity In (so components work well together) and See the Whole (software systems are the product of their interactions).

Putting together these (or similar) agile methods maximizes the effectiveness of the project team and ensures that the delivered product meets the needs of the business or customer.

XP and Lean methods only apply to software projects, DSDM and Scrum can be used on all types of development projects.

# Summary

- Traditional projects start out by specifying and agreeing the requirements; agile projects start out by defining the resources and time frame and allow the required features to evolve through the life of the project
- This book provides an introduction to agile projects, a definition and framework of agile project management, a set of typical agile methods and a description of each phase of an agile project with their deliverables
- Traditional methodology was based on the waterfall model which did not suit projects with poorly defined requirements
- In addition to the problem of trying to fix the requirements too early in a project, traditional methodology also suffered from a lack of customer involvement and an authoritarian approach to managing the project team
- As a result of these problems software developers started evolving lightweight methods such as DSDM, Scrum, Extreme Programming and Lean Development
- This lightweight approach was defined in the Agile Software Manifesto, which was focused on individuals and interactions; working software; customer collaboration; and responding to change
- Trying to manage an agile project with traditional project management methodology proved problematic so the concept of agile project management was born
- A definition of agile project management was published by the DSDM Consortium and this focused on managing a project using the principles of the agile manifesto
- The ideal agile project is a development type project, with poorly defined requirements, a short time frame, a small team and full involvement of the business or customer
- Conversely, large projects, with well defined requirements are probably best managed using traditional methodology
- The typical components of an agile project are therefore likely to include some or all of: agile project management, DSDM, Scrum, Extreme Programming and Lean Development

# 2 Agile Project Management

*This chapter explores the use of agile project management. Starting with the problems of using the traditional approach on an agile project and moving through the benefits and ways of using an agile approach.*

# Traditional Approach

As we saw in the introduction, the traditional approach to project management of software development projects was largely based on principles from the construction industry. This resulted in a waterfall process where first the requirements were fully developed and agreed (strategy), then what would have to be done to meet those requirements was established (analysis), then how it would be done (design) was established, then the solution would be created (build) and finally tested and accepted by the customer.

There already were a number of problems with this approach (many of them becoming visible on high-profile government projects). These problems were further amplified when the same approach was tried on agile projects:

### Requirements

As the requirements are expected to change in an agile project, any processes built on the assumption that the requirements are fully known is doomed to failure. Attempts to overcome this by reverse engineering the requirements from the developed software were cumbersome and difficult to get agreed. Often the solution was to ignore the original requirements documentation completely, which resulted in a badly documented solution.

### Project Plan

In an attempt to plan the project along traditional lines it would be broken down into the traditional stages and these stages would then be broken down into traditional tasks. This resulted in tasks such as 'develop program xyz' but in practice that piece of software was going to change and evolve right through the project so the plan became meaningless.

### Project Success

The Standish Group have been monitoring the success of software projects for many years and still only around 25% are fully successful. The rest are either total failures or severely challenged. The author's own research has shown that the smaller and more agile the project, the more likely it is to be successful.

### Monitoring Progress

The traditional way of monitoring progress is by task completion, typically by tracking them on a Gantt chart. But as we have just seen tasks do not lend themselves to agile development and therefore there will be no accurate progress tracking.

**Beware**

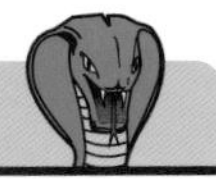

Trying to track progress on an agile project by using traditional methods will not work.

So the traditional approach to managing projects would appear to be incompatible with agile projects. But project management methods have not been standing still and some project managers have already made several steps in the right direction.

## Planning

Good project managers already involve the project team in the detailed planning. For them it would be quite a small step to delegate the planning for the exploration and development phases completely to the developers.

## Organizing

When working on a project involving software development or engineering, good project managers will already be leaving the organization of the detailed technical work to a team leader. This is exactly what is required on an agile project.

## Leading

The best project managers have a good understanding of the needs of the business, they have good communication skills and perhaps most importantly, they have good soft management skills and can delegate well. In fact they are already well on the way to becoming agile project managers.

## Control

Staying in control is all about tracking progress and reporting on it. Good project managers do not micro-manage the team, they trust them to get on with the work and they record progress in the most suitable manner. For an agile project this is by tracking features, iterations and releases completed.

## Communication

As noted under Leading above, good project managers are good communicators. They also ensure that there is good communication within the team and most important of all they make sure there is good communication between the project and the business or customer.

Organizations such as the DSDM Consortium and CC Pace Systems have built on this and mapped out frameworks for agile project management that allow project managers to develop their existing skills in the new agile world. We will be looking at this in the remainder of this chapter.

# The Agile Approach

The aim of the project manager on an agile project is no different than from any other project. To deliver the project on time and to budget and with all the features required by the business. What changes on an agile project is how it is done.

## Planning and Control

The project manager creates the initial, outline, high-level project plan. This will divide the project up into the early phases, followed by the planned product releases. These will then be planned in detail by the by the solution developers and business and consist of a number of iteration timeboxes covering exploration (early prototyping) and engineering (development and testing).

These plans and timeboxes will be agreed with the project manager and reflected back up into the high-level plan. The project manager will be tracking progress by recording the features, iterations and releases delivered and tracking them on a feature burndown chart.

The project manager will be delegating responsibility to the developers and business through the development team leader. The following diagram illustrates the model of this delegation process:

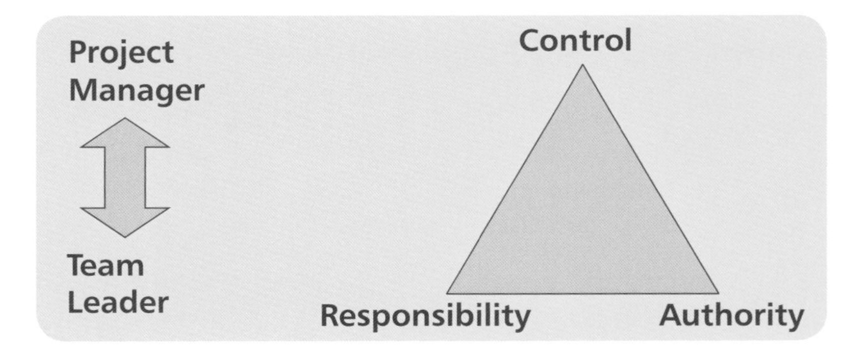


The project manager is responsible to the business for the success of the project while the team leader's job is to carry out the development and deliver a working product. So the project manager delegates responsibility for the development to the team leader. Along with this responsibility the project manager is also delegating the authority to use the relevant resources to carry out the work of the project. You cannot have responsibility for something without the necessary authority to carry it out.

Delegate responsibility and authority but stay in control.

The project manager still has responsibility for the overall control of the project and therefore needs to work with the team leader to record and track progress, deal with issues and problems and report on progress to the business or customer.

## Progress Monitoring

In an agile project there is usually no need for a formal project monitoring system. Progress can be monitored quite simply through the delivery of features and working products. It is, however, important to track the amount of time spent on delivering the products to improve future estimates. Burndown charts showing the number of features delivered and still to be delivered are useful for illustrating the project status.

## Team Motivation

As the development team are self-directing, the project manager's main responsibility is to sustain the team's motivation and morale. If the team does hit problems then the project manager may need to take active steps to improve morale by encouraging or organizing team building or morale boosting events. They will also need to protect the team from external interruptions by dealing with these themselves.

Hot tip

Plan to build in some team building and morale boosting events.

## Business Involvement

Agile development relies on the close and continual involvement of business representatives as part of the development team. The daily stand-up should be planned and take place without fail each day and communication within the team is greatly enhanced by the business representatives and solution developers being located in the same working area.

## Issue Escalation

Any problem or issue that arises in an agile project will be dealt with at the appropriate level. If it is within the scope of the development team (features or issue trade-offs that can be dealt with within the current timebox) they can deal with it through the daily stand-up meeting. If it has wider implications for the project then the project manager should also be involved. But if the issue would cause the project to exceed its time or resource budget or be unable to achieve the required results it will require escalation to the appropriate business decision maker. This will normally be the project sponsor or steering group.

# Agile Framework

CC Pace Systems (www.ccpace.com) developed their Agile Project Management Framework based on the belief that today's project teams are composed of 'knowledge workers' who possess good problem solving ability. The framework is based on six practices for managing agile projects.

## Guiding Vision

At the start of the project the project manager should work closely with the business to understand their vision for the project, how it supports their business goals and how they intend to use it. They should then promote team ownership of this vision through group discussion and facilitation and gently guide the team to keep a focus on the vision.

## Teamwork & Collaboration

By facilitating collaboration and teamwork the project manager will get the best out of the team. The project manager needs to get to know each member of the team as a person and also encourage them to get to know each other. They need to establish an environment in which the team members treat each other with respect. The physical workspace should ideally be open plan with space for individual and common areas. Recognizing success and milestones achieved will all add to the team building effectiveness.

## Simple Rules

The project manager can help the team to establish a simple set of rules that will help them work together. These should be based around the DSDM, Scrum or XP practices as appropriate and can be introduced through a short seminar followed by a team discussion on how best to apply them to the project.

## Open Information

All teams need information to enable them to function but an agile team needs the information to be open and free flowing. They need to know what is going on if they are to be effective. Collective ownership of software code will encourage all the team members to contribute to the project.

Location of the customer representatives with the solution developers will promote an open exchange of information. Daily stand-up meetings will promote the flow of information and the use of information radiators such as project white boards and charts will help to keep everyone fully in the picture.

## Light Touch

Rather than establishing the traditional forms of change control, risk management and people control the project manager should apply just enough control to foster emergent order. Good technical people do not enjoy being micro-managed and left to themselves they would probably be fairly self-controlled as a team. Therefore the project manager should ensure that the team's goals are synchronised with the strategic vision but they should be given enough autonomy to allow them to be innovative and take a creative approach in a fast changing environment.

## Agile Vigilance

The most creativity is said to occur on the border between order and chaos. But the price of this is that the project manager needs to be continually vigilant. Rather than interfering and micro-managing the team the project manager needs to be observant and constantly monitor the team's progress through feedback and tracking the delivery of features, iterations and releases of products.

Implementing this framework can be achieved by the project manager using the following steps:

1. Understand the business's guiding vision and ensure the project team is aligned with it
2. Encourage collaborating and teamwork but also talk to the team members individually. If problems occur be ready to adapt and make changes
3. Having established simple rules with the team, be prepared to be flexible and change them if necessary
4. Make sure information is shared through the daily stand-up meetings, workshops and information radiators
5. Give the team sufficient autonomy so they can be innovative in the way they work
6. Monitor the teams performance in a non-intrusive way

# Business Involvement

The full involvement of the business in an agile project is critical to its success. The collaborative nature of the solution development team means that the people defining the requirements (the business) are working alongside those that are delivering them (the technical team). This enables a rapid response to any changes in requirements and removes the need for formally requesting and documenting any changes.

Make sure the vision and needs of the business are clearly stated and understood by all.

## Business Needs

As we saw in the previous topic, the project manager needs to work closely with the business at the start of the project to fully understand their business vision and needs. Obtaining agreement on these is crucial as every decision made during a project should be made in the light of the main project goal: to deliver what the business needs and when it needs it.

## Business Agreement

The project manager also needs to get the complete business buy-in to the agile approach and philosophy. In order to deliver a working solution when the business needs it, that solution may not include all of the business requirements. It will, however, include all of the top priority requirements and as many of the lower priority requirements as can be included.

The business also needs to commit to providing all of the required human and other resources to the project team. They also need to commit to empowering them to make decisions on the requirements and their priorities.

## Project Sponsor

The most senior business role is that of the project sponsor. They should champion the project to the business. They are the owner of the business case (the justification for the project) and they must be fully supportive of the approach being taken by the project team. They also need to be sufficiently senior in the business to be able to remove obstacles and fix problems that the project might encounter.

## Business Team Members

The business representatives that are assigned to work in the project team are also critical to the success of the project. They will be guiding the developers towards the required business solution. They therefore need to have the knowledge, desire, responsibility and authority to ensure that the solution developed meets the business needs.

## Communication

Another of the project manager's tasks is to make sure that all the team members, whether technical or business, can communicate effectively with one another and any other external sources they need to communicate with. Keeping the size of the team small and having them located together is a tremendous aid to the communication process. The daily stand-up meeting also is crucial to the communication process within the team and the project manager should ensure that it happens.

## Team Size

The ideal size for an agile development team is thought to be between five and nine people. Larger teams will require a greater communications overhead and a more formal approach to communication if they are to be effective. So getting the business agreement to breaking a large team down into smaller, self-sufficient sub-teams will greatly improve their communications and effectiveness.



## Tools and Techniques

If the team is larger and particularly if they are in dispersed locations the project manager will need to take additional steps to ensure there is no breakdown in the communication process. The use of teleconferencing for the daily stand-up and other meetings can prove a great help. Tools are available to allow remote screen sharing for testing and modelling solutions. Getting the team together whenever possible for events like workshops will also be a great help.

Beware

The larger the development team the greater the communication needs.

## Prioritization

Finally the project manager must ensure that the business is fully involved in defining what their requirements are for each timebox as it is planned. They also need to ensure that there are a mix of higher and lower priority requirements so that the team can vary the number of requirements delivered as necessary.

Even having agreed the requirements and their priorities in detail, it is still likely that the business will change its mind about their needs. The project manager needs to be open to these changes while making sure the consequences are understood.

# Team Motivation

In an agile project the solution development team are self-directed and do not require the traditional top down form of project management. In a small close working team every team member will have a good understanding of what is going on. The following table compares the traditional and agile approaches:

| Traditional Projects | Agile Projects |
|---|---|
| Closely managed team | Self-directing team |
| Take directions | Take initiatives |
| Seek individual rewards | Focus on team contributions |
| Concentrate on low level objectives | Concentrate on solutions |
| Competitive | Co-operative |
| Follow processes | Look for better ways of working |
| Reactive | Proactive |

## Motivating the Team

In place of the traditional 'command and control' role, the project manager of an agile project is responsible for the team's motivation and morale. This will not generally be a problem as the team is self-motivating thanks to the rapid progress and continual feedback from the business about the product quality. However, when any problems occur the project manager must be prepared to take any necessary steps to rectify the situation.

As an agile solution development team will consist of technical developers and business representatives working closely together the project manager will need to ensure they collaborate and communicate well.

Traditional project managers who are new to managing agile projects will need to develop their style away from trying to control the team to empowering the team and supporting them. This will mean their spending more time and thought on communication with the team and with each of the individual members of it as well.

By carrying out the following steps the project manager should greatly assist the process of team motivation:

1. Work with the team to define their objectives and then empower the team to achieve them, rather than telling the team how to go about them

2. Ensure that the technical and business members of the team are working in active collaboration, which will positively influence the team's motivation

3. The team needs to be kept stable and the project manager needs to make sure team members are not swapped in and out of the project due to other needs. Specific skills may be needed by the team from time to time and suitably qualified people can be drafted in when required but the core team should remain unchanged

4. Make sure that the team has a stand-up meeting every day and that every team member attends it and actively contributes to it

5. Well planned and well run workshops are an excellent way of team building and improving motivation. They give the team a chance to collaborate on specific topics and use their skills to solve problems and come up with innovative solutions

6. The project manager should protect the team from external interruptions which could deflect them from their work

7. Finally organize team building events and make sure that the team are given frequent rewards to recognise their progress and achievements

**Hot tip**

Effective collaboration will mean the team also produces better work.

**Don't forget**

Remember to build in team and morale boosting events.

# Progress Monitoring

In traditionally managed projects the project manager develops a detailed project plan, usually on a Gantt chart, against which they monitor the completion of tasks or activities. In an agile project there are typically many activities going on in parallel and a different approach to progress monitoring is therefore required.

The things that the project manager can monitor progress on are the release and iteration timeboxes and the features delivered in each. The project manager will also need to monitor the time used on each iteration and release against the resource budget.

## Features

The outline project plan will be produced early in the project and will include a small number of clearly stated requirements. This will be expanded through the subsequent phases of the project into a prioritized requirements list (or features backlog) which will contain all the requirements that the project needs to address.

## Prioritization

Each of these required features needs to be prioritized and the most widely used system is MoSCoW. This stands for Must have, Should have, Could have and Won't have this time. The Must have features are critical and must be included in the release they are planned for. The Could have features will not normally be included unless there is spare capacity. The Should have features should be included but may be dropped by the development team if there is insufficient resource available.

## Feature Burndown

For each product release the team will estimate the number of features that can be included. They will also estimate how many features will be delivered in each iteration. The delivery of these features is referred to as feature burndown.

The feature burndown chart is a graphical representation of the work left to do versus time. There are many variations on this but most feature the outstanding work (backlog) on the vertical axis with time along the horizontal axis.

The chart illustrated at the top of the page opposite is a high-level chart with the planned product releases on the time axis and the planned feature delivery on the work axis. The chart below it takes the next more detailed view of iterations within a product release.

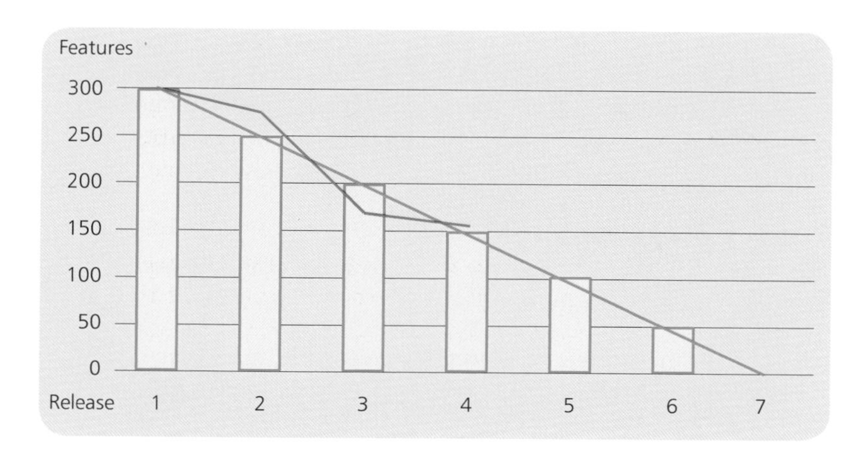


The burndown chart above reflects the strategic project plan with the seven product releases scheduled. The blue bars represent the features backlog at the start of each release. The green line shows the planned feature backlog burndown and the red line shows the actual burndown achieved to date. The chart below is another type of burndown chart for the current release.

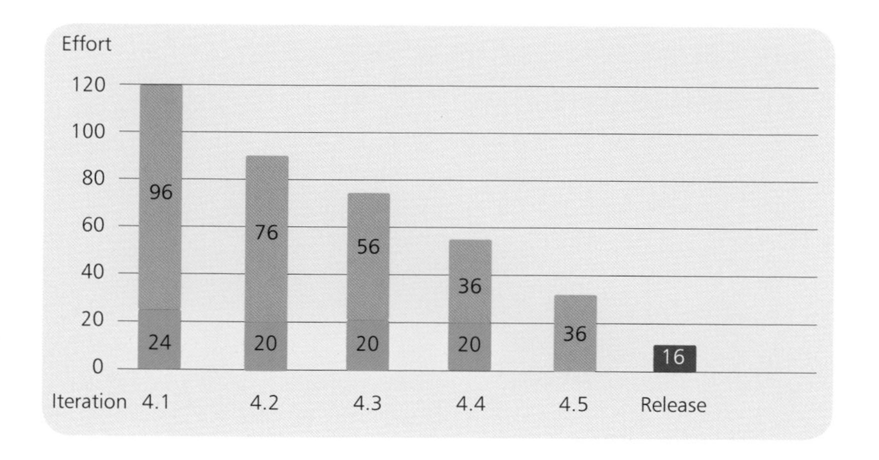


This chart reflects the planned work effort (can be in days, tasks or user stories) burndown for each iteration leading up to the product release. The green bars represent the work completed, the orange bars the work to do and the blue bar the forecast work effort. Project velocity is the measure of how much work gets done on an iteration. This is usually measured in tasks, user stories (cases) or functions delivered.

**Hot tip**

A template for a burndown chart is provided for your use on our website. Go to www.ineasysteps.com/resource-centre/downloads/

**Hot tip**

Project velocity will help make future estimates more accurate.

# Communication

In the preceding topic we looked at the need for the project manager to monitor progress in a way that is realistic on an agile project. By tracking features delivered and the resources used to deliver them the project manager has some key information that will be meaningful to all project stakeholders.

## Project Stakeholders

These are the people who have a vested interest in the outcome of the project. They can include:

- The business: owners, directors, executives, managers and all other employees
- Customers: internal or external and they include anyone who will make use of the output of the project
- The project team: both the solution developers (technical and business) and other members of the project team
- Suppliers: internal or external individuals or groups that provide anything that will be used on the project
- Anyone else: legal, financial, environmental, compliance, government, etc.

## Communication Plan

Once the full list of project stakeholders has been identified we can start to put a communication plan together. This should consist of three things:

- A list of the people we need to communicate with
- Details of what each of them need to know
- The method and frequency of the communication

Hot tip 

A template for a communications plan is provided for your use on our website. Go to www.ineasysteps.com/resource-centre/downloads/

## The Project Team

Communication with and between the members of the project team is critical to the success of the project. Poor communication has often been cited as the most common cause of project failure. So it represents a key aspect of agile project management. One of the most effective ways of communicating with the project team is through meetings and workshops. But the use of information radiators such as notice boards, charts and white boards can also be very effective.

## The Business

Equally if not more important is the business, they are the people the project is being carried out for. In an agile project some members of the business will be embedded with the development team. The other critical member of the business is the project sponsor, who will require a more strategic level of communication. They need to be reassured that everything is going to plan and if not what is being done about it.

## Effective Communication

Communication is critical in an agile project and these are the steps the project manager will need to take for it to be effective:

1. Identify all the project stakeholders and their communication requirements and document this in a communication plan
2. Make sure the team hold a daily stand-up meeting, that they all attend it and contribute to it
3. Communicate progress using information radiators such as charts, graphs and notice boards
4. Use planning workshops to get the team fully involved in planning and taking responsibility for the plans
5. Use velocity tracking to establish the teams capacity for work so they can estimate more accurately based on it
6. Make sure that all members of the team, both technical and business, are communicating effectively
7. Keep the project sponsor in the picture by providing strategic level communication
8. Deliver the level of communication required by other stakeholders in line with the communication plan
9. Review the communication plan from time to time

Hot tip

Never stop effective communication with all the stakeholders.

# Reporting

In addition to meeting some of the communications requirements for project stakeholders, project reports also form a vital control mechanism and record of what is happening when on a project. As a basic agile principle, reports should be fit for purpose and no more. The main reports that will be required during an agile project are time sheets, progress reports, status reports and exception reports plus the end project and benefits assessments.

Hot tip

It is crucial to establish the resources being used early in the project in order to improve future estimates.

### Time Sheets

While never popular, every member of the project team will need to record the time they spend on the project together with the activity or deliverable they were working on. To start with this should be done on a daily basis (if left to the end of the week they may have forgotten half of what they were doing). Initially this is essential for the project manager to track they are getting the resources they require and for the development team to measure their velocity. Once these two factors have been established the requirement can usually be reduced.

### Progress Reports

The team leader should produce a short report from the daily stand-up meeting. A record what was done the previous day, any issues or risks identified and what will be done over the next day.

Don't forget

Keep all reports short and agile: fit for purpose and no more.

The project manager may also produce a summary of what has been done by the development team and by any other team members, including themselves. This will normally be a weekly summary to form a record of the project and also for communication to the team. It may also include charts or graphs of progress and ideally these should also be displayed on notice boards together with other summary information. This is an ideal way of giving the team the big picture.

### Status Reports

The project sponsor and other senior business stakeholders will normally want some form of strategic status report, usually monthly but possibly more frequently on a short but critical project. These reports will normally be in a similar format to the weekly report but at a more strategic level. They should start with a simple statement about the current status of the project and whether it is on track or not and then support it with sufficient detail to justify the initial statement.

Hot tip

A template for a status report is provided for your use on our website. Go to www.ineasysteps.com/resource-centre/downloads/

If there are any issues the report should also say what is being done about them. However, one key thing for the project manager to remember is there should be no surprises in these reports. If there is an issue the project sponsor should already know about it.

Never spring surprises on your project sponsor!

## Escalation Procedure

When problems or issues occur in an agile project they should be dealt with at the lowest level that has the necessary decision making authority. The fact that there is a problem or issue should be reported through the normal channels together with what is being done about it and the eventual resolution.

The development team is the bottom level and if they can resolve the issue it will just get recorded in their daily stand-up reports. However if they cannot deal with the issue it must be escalated using the following steps:

1. The team leader or person that wants to escalate the issue must first check if there is anything they can do about it within their own terms of reference
2. If they cannot resolve the issue the project manager must be notified immediately and an exception report produced
3. Within 48 hours (or as agreed) the project manager and team leader will jointly decide on what will be done. This could involve direct action or further escalation but in either event the decision or actions will be documented

If the project manager cannot resolve the issue they will go through the same three steps above in escalating it to the project sponsor and so on.

## Exception Report

The exception report should contain a description of the current situation with the cause and impact or potential impact on the project. It should set out the alternatives for dealing with the issue, the likely costs, risks and any other impacts. Finally it should recommend which option the team believe is the best to take and why. Once a decision is taken, whether to resolve or further escalate the issue, that should also be added to the report.

Hot tip

A template is provided for your use on our website. Go to www.ineasysteps.com/resource-centre/downloads/

# Summary

- The traditional approach to project management was largely based on principles from the construction industry where requirements were fully developed and agreed right at the start of the project
- This approach often ran into problems when it was applied to software development projects and even more so on agile development projects
- Project management methods have been developing and good project managers are already doing a lot of the things necessary on an agile project
- The agile approach to project management focuses on the empowerment of the solution development team, less formal progress monitoring, team motivation and the full involvement of the business
- The agile project management framework is based on a guiding vision, teamwork and collaboration, simple rules, open information, a light touch and agile vigilance
- Business involvement is critical to the success of an agile project and the project manager should ensure the project remains focused on the business vision and needs
- In an agile project the project manager needs to make sure the team stays motivated by encouraging collaboration, setting team objectives, making sure the team is stable and keeping the team focused
- Progress monitoring on an agile project should focus on the delivery of features against a prioritized list of requirements tracked using burndown charts
- Communication is critical in an agile project, within the team, with the business and with all other stakeholders. The development of a communications plan is a great aid to ensuring adequate communication
- While agile projects are not too formal they still need to capture information on time spent and report progress, plans and issues through short reports

# 3 DSDM

*The Dynamic System Development Method (DSDM) is the only agile method to focus on the management of agile projects. This chapter summarizes the method.*

# DSDM Atern

The Dynamic Systems Development Model (DSDM) was first launched in 1995 by the DSDM Consortium. DSDM Atern is the latest version of the method and is the only agile method to focus on the management of agile projects. Although it was originally developed for software development projects it has subsequently been broadened to cover other types of business change projects.

DSDM provides a framework for developing business solutions in a short time frame while still maintaining quality. Typically the method will prove effective on projects with a time frame of between three to six months.

## Principles

DSDM is based on a number of principles.

- More projects fail because of people issues than because of technology problems
- Nothing is built perfectly the first time and as a rule of thumb 80% of the solution can be produced in 20% of the time it would take to produce the complete solution
- Things can always be completed in a later step if necessary because business requirements will probably change as understanding increases, so any further work could be wasted
- Solutions developed using the method will meet the current needs of the business rather than all perceived possibilities
- Simple solutions that are fit for purpose will be easier to maintain and modify in future

Managing business change and developing solutions for business problems is made more difficult when people from different disciplines and parts of the business need to work together. The DSDM approach deals with some key business problems:

## Communication Problems

Poor communication has been identified as a major cause of project failure. The DSDM model provides a considerable amount of guidance on communication. It also provides an emphasis on human interaction through facilitated workshops, modeling and prototyping, which have all proved more effective than large amounts of documentation.

### Late Delivery

Slipping time scales are a frequent occurrence on traditional projects and preventing them is one of the key problems that DSDM deals with. Being on time is central to the model and that applies to short-term goals as well as the project as a whole. While compromises often have to be made on a project, compromising the deadline is not an option.

### Wrong Solution

Delivering a solution that does not meet the needs of the business is a frequent problem with the traditional approach to projects. Getting a true understanding of the needs of the business is central to the method. DSDM encourages collaboration and good communication. The team are encouraged to embrace change and deal with problems as they occur. They are also encouraged to take on new ideas and develop the solution based on their deepening understanding of the business and its needs.

### Unused Features

Traditionally businesses have tended to over specify their requirements by wanting 'every bell and whistle' that they can think of. This has led to a low percentage of the delivered features actually being used. DSDM maintains a focus on what is important to the business and helps them to prioritize their requirements and only develop features that will be used.

### Changing Requirements

Rather than regarding 'changes of mind' as a problem, the method encourages them and treats changes as good things. It assumes that, with the deeper understanding that comes from developing a solution, a better solution will emerge. With iterative and incremental development and frequent reviews the method understands and plans for change.

### Delayed ROI

Lengthy projects will often result in a delayed or late return on investment (ROI). By using incremental delivery the business can start to benefit from the evolving solution as early as possible.

### Gold Plating

Over-engineering or trying to make a solution perfect can produce an ever diminishing return. Prioritization ensures that the business gets something good enough in a window of opportunity.

**Hot tip**

The solution needs to be fit for purpose, any more is waste.

# Principles

DSDM Atern is based on eight principles which guide the team in the attitude and mind set they should adopt.

### Focus on the Business Need

- Understand the true business priorities
- Establish a sound business case
- Seek continuous business sponsorship and commitment
- Guarantee to produce the key (top priority) deliverables

### Deliver on Time

- Timebox the work
- Focus on the priorities of the business
- Always hit deadlines

### Collaborate

- Involve the right stakeholders, at the right time, throughout the project
- Ensure the members of the team are empowered to take decisions on behalf of those they represent
- Actively involve the business representatives
- Build a one-team culture

### Never Compromise on Quality

- Determine the required level of quality at the start
- Make sure that quality does not become a variable
- Design, document and test appropriately
- Build quality in by constant review
- Test early and test continuously

### Build Incrementally

- Strive for early delivery of business benefit where possible

- Continually confirm that the correct solution is being built
- Formally re-assess priorities and project viability with each increment delivered

## Develop Iteratively

- Do enough design up front to create a strong foundation
- Take an iterative approach to building all products
- Build customer feedback into each iteration
- Accept that most details emerge later rather than sooner
- Embrace change to get the right solution
- Be creative, experiment, learn and evolve

## Communicate Continuously

- Run daily team stand-up sessions
- Use facilitated workshops
- Use techniques such as modeling and prototyping
- Present the evolving solution early and often
- Keep documentation lean and timely
- Manage stakeholder expectations throughout the project
- Encourage informal face-to-face communication

## Demonstrate Control

- Use an appropriate level of formality for tracking and reporting progress
- Make plans and progress visible to everyone
- Measure progress through delivery of products rather than completed activities
- Manage proactively
- Evaluate continuing project viability based on business objectives

# Project Lifecycle

The DSDM Atern project lifecycle is both iterative and incremental as defined in the fifth and sixth principles. The solution will be delivered to the business through a series of increments that will each build on the previous release by adding to and making improvements to the functionality. The project lifecycle is illustrated in the following diagram:

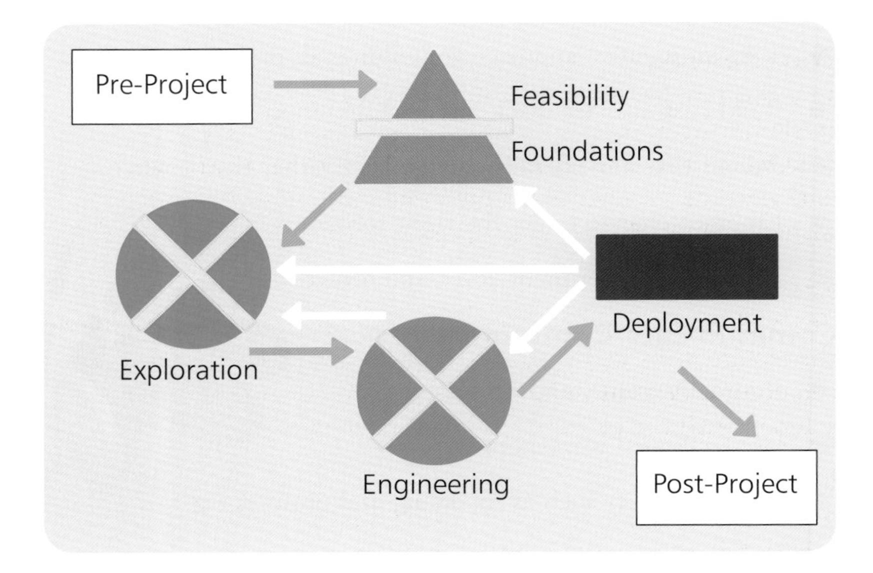


The project process as illustrated above, consists of five project phases: Feasibility, Foundations, Exploration, Engineering and Deployment. They are preceded by a Pre-Project phase and followed by a Post-Project phase.

The main path through the lifecycle is illustrated by the green arrows but as it is iterative and incremental, following the deployment of each release, the project can return to the engineering, exploration or foundations phase for the start of the next release.

## Pre-Project

The pre-project phase is to make sure that only the right projects get started and that they are set up correctly. It describes the business problem to be addressed, identifies the project sponsor and business visionary and confirms that the project is aligned to the business strategy. It also provides the terms of reference, plan and resources for the feasibility phase.

### Feasibility

The feasibility phase examines the viability of the project by establishing whether there is a feasible solution to the business problem and the likely benefits that it will provide. It outlines the possible approaches for delivering the solution, the type of project team that will be required and the initial estimates for the project timescale and cost.

### Foundations

In a small project the foundations phase can be combined with feasibility. Its purpose is to produce the baseline high-level requirements for the project together with the business case and schedule. It outlines the proposed solution with its project management, technical, quality, risk and lifecycle elements.

### Exploration

The exploration phase will iteratively and incrementally investigate the requirements and produce models and prototypes of a viable solution for demonstration to the business. These preliminary solutions will not be fully functional or robust.

### Engineering

The engineering phase turns the preliminary solution into a robust, fully-functional business solution.

### Deployment

The deployment phase brings the solution into live use in the business, providing training and support for the end users where needed. It also acts as a review of the product and functionality delivered so far, with an assessment of the benefits delivered against the business case. Finally it should decide whether the project should continue with further interim releases or should now be closed as it has delivered sufficient benefit and the cost of further development would outweigh any further benefit.

Following the final deployment the project will be closed and reviewed from a technical and business perspective.

### Post-Project

Around six months after the end of the project (or when the business benefits can actually be measured) the post-project review should examine whether the business benefits, as set out in the business case, have been met by the deployed solution.

**Hot tip** 

This lifecycle can be configured to meet the needs of each project and multiple exploration and engineering phases can be run in parallel if needed.

# Roles & Responsibilities

A cornerstone of the DSDM method is that the business or customer is fully involved in the development of the solution with the developers or supplier side of the project. The diagram below illustrates the project roles from the business (orange), project management (blue) and technical (green) backgrounds.

| | | | |
|---|---|---|---|
| Project Management | Business Sponsor | Project Manager | Technical Co-ordinator |
| | Business Visionary | | |
| Solution Development | Business Analyst | | Team Leader |
| | Business Advisor | Workshop Facilitator | Solution Developer |
| | Business Ambassador | DSDM Coach | Solution Tester |



## Business Sponsor

This is the most senior project role. The project sponsor is the champion of the project and must be a senior business executive with sufficient authority to resolve any business issues. They are responsible for the business case, the on-going viability of the project and making sure that funds and other resources are made available to the project.

## Project Manager

Responsible for all aspects of delivering the solution to the business. Co-ordinates all aspects of managing the project but leaves the detailed level of planning the product delivery to the members of the solution development team.

## Technical Co-ordinator

The technical design authority for the project. They are also responsible for ensuring the solution development team function effectively and meet the desired technical and quality standards.

## Business Visionary

More actively involved than the project sponsor, the business visionary is responsible for interpreting the needs of the sponsor, communicating these to the team and ensuring they are properly represented in the business case.

### Team Leader

Reporting to the project manager, the team leader co-ordinates the work of the solution development team and ensures that the products are delivered on time. In addition they will often perform another role such as business analyst or solution developer.

### Business Analyst

This role is of particular relevance to IT projects and is the link between the business and the solution developers. Responsible for ensuring that the business needs are properly understood and correctly reflected in the solution developed.

### Solution Developer

Interprets the business requirements and produces a deployable solution to them that meets the functional and non-functional needs of the business. Develops models, prototypes and deployable solutions and documents changes to the requirements.

### Solution Tester

Works with the business roles to define the test scenarios and test cases that will be used for testing the evolving solution. Performs tests on the developing solution and reports on the results.

### Business Advisor

Called upon to provide specific or specialist input to the solution developers and testers. They will often be an intended user of the solution but may also provide technical input of business rules or regulations.

### Business Ambassador

A representative of the business area that will use the solution. Their role is to provide information on the business use of the solution and its suitability for purpose. They must have the responsibility and knowledge necessary to ensure that the right solution is delivered to meet the business needs.

### Workshop Facilitator

Responsible for the planning, preparation and communication of workshops but not their content.

### DSDM Coach

Responsible for helping a team with limited experience of the method to become effective in its use.

**Hot tip**

Several of these roles may be provided by the same person, particularly in a smaller project.

# Facilitated Workshops

Workshops, facilitated by an independent person with no vested interest in the outcome, are a powerful tool for harnessing the strength of the team. They need to have a clear objective (the product) and the attendees need to be empowered to produce the product.

## Benefits

Facilitated workshops can have a number of direct and indirect benefits to the project.

- Fast, high quality decision making as they can shorten the amount of time needed to get agreement and acceptance on requirements and other key deliverables
- Improved stakeholder buy-in as the participants feel more involved and committed to the outcome and more enthusiastic about the project
- Team building through the synergy and understanding that will develop as the participants build on each others' ideas
- Consensus can be achieved on key decisions and good buy-in from the participants should result
- Issues can be clarified and ambiguities and misunderstandings can be prevented leading to a better product

Hot tip

SWOT charts are used to record strengths, weaknesses, opportunities and threats

## Workshop Process

The facilitator should plan the processes to be used in advance. Techniques such as brain-storming, story boards, mind maps, diagrams and SWOT charts all work well in workshops supported by tools such as flip charts, white boards and sticky notes.

## Workshop Facilitator

The facilitator's role is to manage the workshop process and guide the participants through to the achievement of their goal. They will also need to make sure everyone contributes and no one dominates too much. The roles of the other workshop participants are as follows:

## Workshop Owner

The owner of the workshop is the person who will own the deliverables from it. They should be involved in the definition of the objective and the resourcing of the workshop.

## Participants

The participants are the people who are needed to achieve the objective and produce the product. They should have the necessary knowledge and skills and be empowered to make decisions.

## Workshop Scribe

The scribe keeps a record of the workshop outcomes, decisions taken and follow-on actions agreed.

## Workshop Activities

The workshop facilitator will need to carry out the following steps to run a successful workshop:

1. Define the objectives with the workshop owner and plan the workshop and participants accordingly
2. Prepare for the workshop by distributing the agenda, objectives and any other details to all the participants
3. Run the workshop by outlining the ground rules that will be followed and then getting it under way
4. Review the workshop with the participants at the end, noting whether it achieved its objectives and any lessons learned for future workshops
5. Distribute the scribe's workshop report which should document decisions, actions, issues and the product of the workshop itself
6. Follow-up the workshop with the workshop owner to confirm the results and note any follow on actions that need to be addressed

## Success Factors

Factors that make for a successful workshop are: an independent experienced workshop facilitator; clearly defined objectives; good preparation; a method for talking in lessons learned from previous workshops; not forcing the participants to reach a decision; and distributing the workshop report soon after the event.

# Prioritization

As the main variable on an agile project is the requirements, it stands to reason that these requirements must be prioritized so that the ones that really matter to the business get dealt with. The most straight forward method of prioritization is MoSCoW.

## MoSCoW Rules

These rules should be agreed with the business users before the requirements gathering starts. The requirements are categorized into Must have, Should have, Could have and Won't have this time. The definition of each category is as follows:

## Must Have

The must have requirements are the features that have to be included in the delivered solution. Failure to deliver any of them would mean the solution would be unusable and the business case would not be met. They form the minimum usable subset which the project guarantees to deliver.

## Should Have

The should have requirements are deemed to be important to the business but not vital. While there may be some pain if they are not included the solution would still be viable. Their exclusion may involve the need for some form of work around or may make the solution less efficient or effective.

## Could Have

The could have requirements are desirable features but less critical than the should have requirements. Leaving them out will have less impact on the business than the should haves.

## Won't Have This Time

The won't have requirements are those that the project team has agreed not to deliver. They are still documented as they help to clarify the scope of the project and they may still make it into the solution on a later release.

Having agreed the definition of these categories of requirements with the business, it is then up to the business to justify why any particular requirement is a must have. Following each release of the solution all the remaining unsatisfied requirements should be re-prioritized for the next release. Requirements can be promoted or demoted according to how critical they are to the next release of the solution.

As a rough rule of thumb the must have requirements should not exceed 60% of the total effort of the project. This results in an effective contingency of 40% of the total effort of the project. Assuming the should haves and could haves are split equally this means it is quite likely that the should haves can be included and still have a 20% contingency.

At the start of a project the requirements will be very high level and will probably all be must haves. During the project the requirements will be broken down into lower level requirements and at this stage the other categories should start to be assigned.

## Assigning Priorities

As an approach to assigning priorities first make sure the business is fully on board with the MoSCoW rules and then:

1. Start out with all the requirements defined as Won't Haves and get the business to justify why they need them
2. Challenge all Must Haves to ensure they are show stoppers and not just nice to haves
3. Find out why each requirement is needed for the project or the next release of the solution
4. If there is more than one requirement implied in any requirement, decompose it, then check if they are all the same priority or even needed
5. Every requirement should be traceable to a project objective, if the objective is not a must have then the requirement shouldn't be either
6. Remember that priorities can change, so re-evaluate them after each release of the solution
7. Any defects should also be prioritized using MoSCoW

Remember that if you have any more than 60% must haves it will pose a serious risk to the success of the project.

**Hot tip**

Challenge all must haves and make the business justify them.

# Iterative Development

Iterative development is fundamental to evolving the solution from the initial high level requirement to a delivered product. The DSDM iterative development process follows a cycle of: Identify, Plan, Evolve and Review as illustrated below:

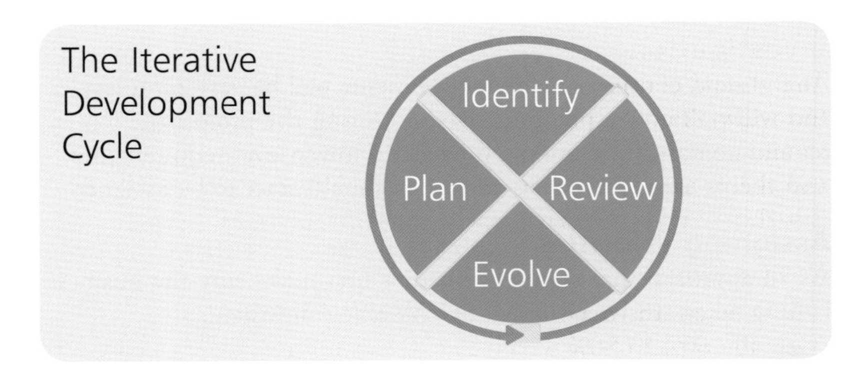


### Identify

During this part of the cycle the solution development team agree the objectives for whatever it is that they are developing.

### Plan

The team then agree what needs to be done and by whom in order to meet the objectives they have defined.

### Evolve

Next the planned activities are carried out by the team in the agreed timebox.

### Review

Finally the results of the activities are reviewed to see if the objectives have been achieved. If they have been achieved then the changes are accepted and the cycle begins again by identifying the objectives for the next cycle and so on.

If the objectives have not been met the team will either:

- Reject the changes and go back to the previous version, or
- Identify the remedial work that will be required to meet the objectives

In either event a new cycle will begin by identifying the objectives for the next cycle.

## Managing the Process

Overall management of the iterative development process is through the use of timeboxing, change control, configuration management, quality assurance and testing. The method recommends the use of three iterations:

### Investigation

This should consist of a single pass round the development cycle to review all of the products to be evolved in the timebox. This should give the team a good understanding of the requirements and the potential solutions to be developed. As a rule of thumb this should typically take 10% to 20% of the total timebox.

### Refinement

This is where the majority of the work will be carried out (typically 60% to 80% of the total timebox). The work is driven by the priorities established at the start of the timebox and by the learnings to emerge from the investigation iteration.

### Consolidation

During this iteration the team work to complete as many of the deliverables as possible within the MoSCoW priorities. This will be based on the results of the review at the end of the refinement iteration. Again as a rule of thumb this should typically take 10% to 20% of the total timebox.

## Development Strategy

The prioritized requirements list should be developed in the foundations phase of the project and fed into the planning for evolution and engineering. The method defines three strategies for developing the requirements:

A vertical approach where requirements are delivered sequentially so that something basic is available early on and features are fully completed at the end of each timebox.

A horizontal approach where the requirements are evolved in parallel. So all the requirements are addressed early but in a fairly simplistic way. Each subsequent timebox fills them out until they are fully met.

A combined approach where all the requirements are addressed in a simplistic way. This gives an early view of the full solution, then each requirement is fully developed sequentially.

# Modeling & Prototyping

Most types of development projects can benefit from the use of storyboards, models and prototypes to help establish the requirements and check the suitability of the proposed solution. These can be anything from throw-away mock-ups of the proposed solution to prototypes that might be further evolved into the delivered solution.

## Models

A model is typically used to help visualize something which does not yet exist. It may be a scaled-down replica of a building, a set of illustrations or dummy screen shots or a partially working software prototype that will eventually be engineered into the solution.

## Abstraction

Most models include some level of abstraction, as some detail is left out to allow the audience to focus on the particular purpose of the model. Prototypes will normally have a reduced function set or some of the functionality will not work as eventually intended.

When developing models and prototypes it is important to set the audience's expectations about the level of abstraction so they focus on the purpose of the model. Models and prototypes play a different role during the different project phases as follows:

## Pre-Project

In the pre-project phase models of the existing or previous solution may help to clarify the issues. A very basic model of the initial thoughts about a solution may help to clarify the objectives of the proposed project.

## Feasibility

During feasibility the model will typically be trying to define the scope of the project. The terms of reference will help to define why the project is being carried out. Basic models could illustrate the different options being considered.

## Foundations

In the foundations phase the focus of the team is on the identification, definition and prioritization of requirements. Models can help to illustrate the scope of the required solution and also the different solution options. High-level diagrams may also assist in establishing the foundations of the project.

## Exploration

The exploration phase is an incremental one, where the team develop and evolve more and more detailed models of the proposed solution.

## Engineering

During the engineering phase the models will be turned into prototypes as the full technical solution begins to evolve. This will continue through the many iterations as the prototypes evolve into the fully working solution for deployment.

## Use of Models

Models and prototypes are a significant aid to communication between the development team and the business. Models can be anything from sticky notes to a nearly fully-functional solution. The following steps will improve the modeling process:

1. Develop models iteratively by taking a top-down approach to details and modeling from different perspectives to aid understanding
2. Models should always assist the communication process and not become a pointless burden on the project
3. Make sure to use appropriate language that the audience will understand to describe the models
4. The models developed should be appropriate for the project and the abilities of the team to develop them
5. DSDM does not have any rules for models, use whatever works for the project and the organization
6. Models should initially communicate the big picture and then progressively break it down to more manageable chunks that can be developed incrementally
7. Finally don't forget to have fun, developing models can and should be an enjoyable experience for the team and the business

Models are a very effective way of communicating a proposed solution.

# Timeboxing

In DSDM timeboxing is a key technique for controlling the delivery of products in an iterative environment. Used with prioritized requirements it can ensure that each timebox is completed on time and every time.

## Timebox Control

Each timebox starts with a kick-off meeting and ends with a close out meeting. In between these the timebox passes through three stages or iterations: investigation, refinement and consolidation.

## Kick Off

This short meeting starts with the solution development team reviewing the timebox objectives and confirming that they are still achievable. They then agree the acceptance criteria for each of the products being delivered. The availability of team members to do the necessary work is confirmed together with any external dependencies and the risks of their non-availability. Finally the team should ensure they have a mix of priority requirements in line with the MoSCoW rules.

## Investigation Iteration

During the investigation, which should typically take 10% to 20% of the timebox, the solution developers will work closely with the business ambassadors investigating the requirements and how best they can be met. Where possible an initial prototype of the solution should be created to communicate the proposed solution.

## Refinement Iteration

The majority of the development work (typically 60% to 80%) will be carried out in this stage. The work will be divided up and the priorities and delivery schedule agreed. As much of the work as possible will then be completed, including testing. The refinement iteration then ends with a review of the work and what is needed to achieve completion. No new work should be started after this point and any changes requested should be prioritized.

## Consolidation Iteration

In the consolidation stage any actions agreed at the review are carried out together with any further work to ensure the products meet their acceptance criteria. Quality assurance is then performed to confirm the products meet the required standard and are fit for purpose. Any products which fail in this respect are deemed not to have been delivered.

## Close Out

The purpose of the close out meeting is to record the formal acceptance by the business of the products delivered by the timebox. It also has to decide what to do about any work that was included in the timebox but was not completed. This work can be considered for a future timebox or dropped completely. Finally the timebox should be reviewed for any lessons learned to be passed on to future timeboxes.

If practical the close out meeting could then run back to back with the kick off for the next timebox.

## Daily Stand-Up

The team working on a timebox should meet every day for a short stand-up meeting. This will normally be run by the team leader and it is a daily chance to understand the team's progress towards its objectives and any issues that have been encountered. It is a short meeting of no more than 15 minutes held in the team's work place.

Each team member has a couple of minutes to say what they have been doing since the last stand-up, what they will be doing until the next stand-up and any issues (problems) or risks they have encountered. It is the way the team leader tracks progress and controls the work of the team.

## Change Control

As the products of the timebox are constantly being refined by team review it is essential that the team members and particularly the business ambassador have the authority to make decisions about changes. So there is no formal change control process in place as long as any changes are within the agreed scope.

## Timebox Scheduling

The overall delivery plan will provide a schedule of the increments and within each of these the timeboxes that will make up the increments. The schedule should therefore show the number and duration of each timebox in the current increment.

Using the timebox technique set out in this topic with prioritized requirements will ensure that each timebox is completed on time. This will mean the increment will also be completed on time and likewise the project itself.

# Estimating

In traditional project management the work has to be estimated so that the schedule can be produced. In DSDM it is the other way around, the schedule is produced and then the work has to be estimated so that we can plan how many of the requirements can be produced in the given timeframe. There are four key points to be considered in estimating for an agile project:

- Estimates need to include an element of contingency to deal with the unknown and that is done by including Should and Could have requirements as well as Must haves
- Estimates only need to be as accurate as is necessary for their purpose at any stage of a project
- Wherever possible the estimates should be produced by the people delivering the solution
- Estimates should be reviewed and revised throughout the project as knowledge of the requirements increases and the team's velocity becomes established

During Feasibility the estimates will be based on very limited knowledge. During Foundations more detail will become known and as the solution begins to be developed in Exploration and Engineering more information will become known together with a measure of velocity. The estimates will get more and more accurate through the project.

## Contingency

In DSDM contingency is added by the prioritization of the features rather than by adding additional time to tasks. Because of this, work estimates must include sufficient low priority features to provide the required level of contingency. The result of this is that the Must Haves should only account for around 50% of the requirements in the early stages and 60% later.

## Producing Estimates

Estimates should be produced and owned by the people who will be doing the actual work. They should be based on whatever information is currently available and sufficient low priority features should be included. They must be produced in collaboration with the business and they should be recorded with any assumptions and risks. Then the actual outcome can be compared to the estimates and any lessons learned.

## Estimating Process

The very early estimates are likely to be produced by assessing the overall size of the project based on previous experience. Further into the project it needs to be broken down or decomposed into its component parts. Traditionally this was by tasks but it could be requirements, features, use cases, products or components.

Whatever the components are, they then need to be sized and the effort required to produce each needs to be estimated. This is where the team need to be involved as they will usually have some experience of doing something similar.

## Estimating Workshops

We have already looked at facilitated workshops in an earlier topic and estimating is an ideal application for a series of workshops. Early in the project the participants will be selected for their business and technical knowledge. Then at the start of each timebox the development team can revise and refine the estimates based on their actual experience to date.

## Presenting Estimates

Early in the project the estimates will be theoretical, based on 'best guess' and 'past experience'. The safest way of presenting these estimates is as a range that shows the level of confidence in the estimate.

Early estimates should be rounded and should reflect a low level of confidence (e.g. 100 to 200 days/$250,000 to $500,000). One way of achieving this is to define the bottom of the range as the estimated time and cost of delivering only the must have requirements, the mid-point should then be the estimated time and cost of delivering the should and could haves as well and the top end should be the same as the difference between the bottom and mid point.

Further into the project the estimating will get more accurate as the requirements are better understood and the range of time and costs will not need to be so extreme. The bottom of the range will still be the time and cost of delivering the must haves but the top end will be the cost of delivering the should have and could haves as well. Once into timeboxing the duration and resources are set and the estimates of features delivered will get more and more accurate based on the team's experience to date.

Hot tip

Presenting estimates as a range is always better than a single figure.

# Quality

The quality of the solution that is delivered by the project will be judged on whether or not it is fit for purpose. That is whether or not it meet the needs of the business. This will include the delivery of the minimum usable subset of the requirements (the must haves), the operability and performance (non-functional requirements) and that it can be maintained by the business.

The business may also have quality management standards that the project has to adhere to. These could include project governance, project management guidelines or standards, ISO processes, industry compliance regulations, documentation standards and so on.

## Defining Quality

If the quality of the delivered solution is to be judged as fit for purpose, then the required quality must be defined and agreed at the start of the project. This definition once agreed, is what must be achieved for the solution to be fit for purpose. If quality is not defined and agreed adequately is can result in several problems with the delivered solution:

- It fails to meet the needs of the business
- It contains the wrong functionality
- It has too many errors
- It is difficult, time consuming and costly to support
- It is overly complex and difficult to use

If quality together with the functional and non-functional requirements are all agreed at the start of the project, then there will be a common understanding of what is required. Quality then becomes an integral part of all plans and these problems will be avoided.

## Maintainability

Part of the on-going cost of operating any new system or process is the cost of maintenance. But making a product easy to maintain may well increase the cost and duration of the project, so there may need to be some sort of trade off. DSDM suggests one of three levels of maintainability:

- Maintainability is a required attribute of the initial solution

- Deliver a working solution as soon as possible, then re-engineer the solution for maintainability afterwards
- Deliver a short-term working solution as soon as possible

Once the maintainability has been defined it should be re-confirmed at all the major development milestones.

## Quality Management

One thing that should not happen on an agile project is that the quality management process starts to interfere with the business focus of the project. Formal quality reviews and sign-offs should not be needed. Quality is measured through the business acceptance of deliverables as being fit for purpose. However the project should be able to demonstrate that:

- Correct processes are being followed
- Appropriate deliverables are being produced
- Everyone knows who is responsible for what
- Everyone knows what will happen next

The business involvement in the review and acceptance of deliverables should ensure they are appropriate. The other aspects are achieved through good communication.

## Quality Reviews

If quality is to be reviewed during the project, then these reviews must be included in the planning. Every planning session, therefore, should include quality and how it will be reviewed against the plan. In an agile project these reviews should not result in additional or unnecessary work and would typically cover:

- Is the team sufficiently empowered?
- Is there sufficient business involvement?
- Are the products being produced and priorities adhered to?
- Is the life-cycle being followed?
- Are the timeboxes being respected?
- Is feedback from reviews being incorporated?

# Risk Management

The management of risk is an on-going process that should be started early in the project and continue throughout the project life-cycle. Risks are things that threaten the project and the achievement of its objectives. They could be severe threats that would result in the whole project being cancelled or minor threats that might cause a small delay or mean changing a deliverable. But they all need to be identified, evaluated and have suitable counter-measures planned for them as illustrated below:

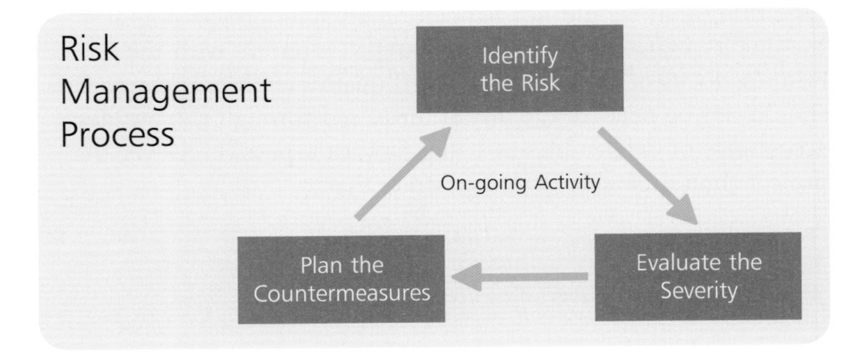


## Risks in Agile Projects

Agile projects address some of the key risks that are encountered in traditional projects such as missed deadlines and changing requirements. But they introduce others risks such as their dependence on full business involvement and a small development team (loss of any team members could cause problems). In addition to these, there are all the usual things that can go wrong with a project such as supplier failure or technical issues.

## Risk Identification

It is never too early to start identifying project risks. The project terms of reference and business case may already have identified some but that is just the start. Once the project team is assembled a risk workshop using simple brain-storming and flip charts is an excellent way of identifying risks. Then every time a plan is produced, at any level, part of the process should be considering the risks.

## Risk Log

Having started to identify the risks to the project they need to be recorded in some form of risk log. This need not be anything very complex, just a record of the risk and who 'owns' it. Then further details can be added as it is evaluated and countermeasures are planned.

## Risk Evaluation

The process of evaluating the severity of the risk should follow on from its identification. The simplest (and arguably most effective) way of evaluating risks is to consider the impact and probability and rate them as low, medium or high.

High probability would indicate that it is very likely to happen, medium that it is a 50/50 chance, and low that it is unlikely to happen.

High impact would indicate a serious threat to the project's continuation, medium that there would be some pain in terms of delays or loss of functionality and low that it would be an irritation but not pose a serious threat.

## Countermeasures

Having evaluated the severity of the risk, then the necessary countermeasures can be considered. Traditionally these are considered to be:

- Prevention: this will usually be the most costly option and will only be used where a risk must be prevented at all costs
- Reduction: taking steps to reduce the probability or to reduce the impact if the risk does happen are usually less costly
- Acceptance: sometimes there is not anything that can be done about a risk so the business just accepts it
- Transfer: sometimes the risk can be transferred to a supplier, and insurer or someone else within the business
- Contingency Plan: often in conjunction with one or more of the above a plan will be prepared for what will be done if the risk does occur.

## Continual Monitoring

The essence of risk management is that it does not stop. Risks will change with time and according to the phase of the project. That is the key reason for recording them in the risk log and tracking what is being done about them and by whom.

# Summary

- DSDM provides a framework for developing business solutions in a short time-frame while still maintaining quality
- DSDM helps to prevent poor communications, late delivery, wrong solution, unused features, changing requirements, delayed ROI and gold plating.
- It is based on eight principles: focus on the business need; deliver on time; collaborate; never compromise on quality; build incrementally; develop iteratively; communicate continuously; and demonstrate control
- The project life-cycle has five phases: feasibility, foundations, exploration, engineering and deployment. These are preceded by a pre-project and followed by a post-project phase
- The method defines thirteen different roles from the business sponsor down to the workshop facilitator and DSDM coach
- Facilitated workshops are a powerful tool for harnessing the strength of the team
- The MoSCoW Rules prioritize requirements as: Must have, Should have, Could have and Won't have this time
- The iterative development cycle consists of four stages: identify (to set the objectives), plan (what is going to be done), evolve (carry out the plan) and review (the results)
- Models, prototypes, storyboards and other techniques provide a rich method of communicating requirements and proposed solutions
- Timeboxing is the mechanism for controlling the delivery time while allowing the number of requirements to vary
- Estimating consists of working out how much of the requirements can be delivered in the available time
- Quality requirements need to be defined at the start of the project and reviewed in a non-intrusive way
- Although agile projects do reduce some traditional risks, they also introduce some risks through their dependence on the collaboration between the business and the developers

# 4 Scrum

*Scrum provides one of the most popular agile methods for developing complex products. It builds on and has been proved to work well with other agile components.*

# Scrum Overview

Scrum is an iterative, incremental framework for managing product development. Although it is most often used in software development projects it is also applicable to other types of development projects

## Background

Hirotaka Takeuchi and Ikujiro Nonaka first described a new approach to the development of commercial products that would give increased speed and flexibility in 1986. They referred to this as a rugby approach as it is performed by a cross-functional team that "tries to go the distance as a unit, passing the ball back and forth" very similar to a game of rugby.

The term Scrum started being used to describe the approach in the early 1990's. In rugby a Scrum is the method of restarting the game after a minor infringement. Finally Ken Schwaber and Jeff Sutherland collaborated in the late 1990s and on into the 2000s to produce a definitive guide to Scrum methodology and the rules of the game. This chapter summarizes their approach along with some helpful input from other practitioners.

## Scrum

They define a Scrum as "a framework within which people can address complex problems, while productively and creatively delivering products of the highest possible value". The framework and terminology are simple concepts and easy to understand and yet they are difficult to implement.

It is important to understand that Scrum is only a framework for managing complex product development. It is not a technique or process for building products. For this reason it works well with software development techniques such as Extreme Programming (XP) and Lean Development. It also interfaces well with DSDM and Agile Project Management.

## Scrum Framework

The Scrum framework consists of the team (and the individual roles within it), the events that take place (sprint planning, daily scrum, sprint reviews and sprint retrospective), the artifacts (product backlog, sprint backlog and burndown chart) and the rules of the game (how the roles, events and artifacts interact). Most of the events and artifacts are very similar to those defined in DSDM and Agile Project Management.

Scrum fits well with Agile Project Management and DSDM as well as with XP and Lean Development.

## The Team

There are a number of roles within the team:

- Product Owner: who is responsible for the business value of the product
- Scrum Master: who ensures that the team is both functional and productive
- Team: the self-organized group who get the work done (which would include similar roles to those defined in DSDM and Agile Project Management)

Hot tip

Successful teams embrace the values on which Scrum is built, as enshrined in the Agile Manifesto.

## The Events

There are four events central to the Scrum framework:

- Sprint Planning: where the team meets with the product owner to select the set of features that will be delivered during a sprint
- Daily Scrum: as the name suggests a daily stand-up meeting where the team share their progress and problems
- Sprint Reviews: the team demonstrate what they have completed to the product owner
- Sprint Retrospective: where the team look back at what they did and forward for ways to improve the product or the process they are using

## The Artifacts

There are three artifacts:

- Product Backlog: the prioritized requirements list of desired project outcomes (features)
- Sprint Backlog: a selected sub-set of work from the product backlog that the team agrees to complete in a sprint, broken down into tasks
- Burndown Chart: a visual interpretation of the progress showing the work remaining. Often there will be two burndown charts maintained: one for the overall project and one for the current sprint

The Scrum rules are described in the remainder of this chapter.

# Scrum Theory

Scrum theory is based on the experiential learning circle. This states that knowledge and understanding come from a process of planning something, doing it, reviewing how it worked and then adapting the process to be used the next time

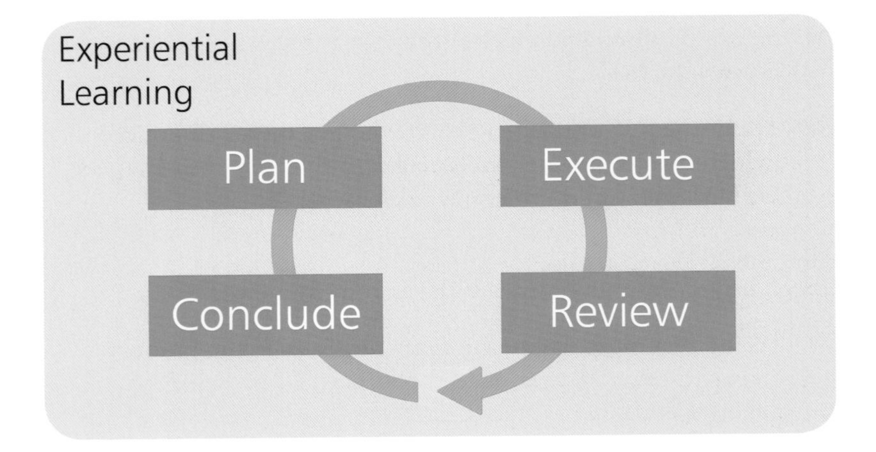


As Scrum employs an iterative, incremental process it fits this model at two levels:

- At the sprint level the four stages equate to sprint planning, executing the development work, the sprint review and sprint retrospective
- At the daily work level the four stages equate to the daily scrum, executing the tasks and the review and conclusions come in the following daily scrum

Scrum theory is based on the three pillars of transparency, inspection and adaptation.

## Transparency

In Scrum the process being used must be fully visible to everyone in the team. The standards being used must be common and again understood by everyone on the team. Finally the language used to describe the process must be shared by the team.

The example of the need for a common understanding of language most often quoted is the definition of the word 'Done'. This clearly must be shared and agreed by those doing the work and those inspecting and accepting it.

## Inspection

In Scrum the development work and artifacts being produced must be inspected frequently in order to identify any variations from the desired goal. These inspections should be done in such a way that they do not obstruct the ongoing work. They are, however, best done with due diligence by skilled inspectors at the actual point of work.

## Adaptation

Following an inspection, if it is deemed that one or more aspects of the process have deviated outside of acceptable levels of tolerance and that the resulting product would be unacceptable, the process or the product will need to be adjusted. That adjustment has to be made as soon as possible to reduce the risk of further deviation.

Scrum defines four formal events where there are opportunities for such inspection and adaptation:

- Sprint Planning
- Daily Scrum
- Sprint Review
- Sprint Retrospective

## Scrum Framework

Scrum provides a framework that is designed to support the development of complex products and consists of:

- Scrum Teams: which are self-contained, cross-functional teams containing all of the skills required to develop the required products
- Scrum Events: sprint planning, daily scrum, sprint review and sprint retrospective
- Scrum Artifacts: the product backlog, sprint backlog and burn down charts

Each of these three components has its purpose and is critical to the success of the framework. The way that they interact and are bound together is described by the rules of the game, which are set out in the remainder of this chapter.

Hot tip

The Rules of the Game are not set out as one topic but are interspersed in the remainder of the chapter.

# Scrum Team

The Scrum Team is a self-contained, cross-functional team that contains all of the skills and knowledge required to develop the required products. The Scrum Team is also self-organizing so they can choose how they go about the necessary work.

As they are working iteratively and incrementally, the Scrum Team aim to deliver a usable working version of products on every iteration and release. The Scrum Team consists of the product owner and development team and is facilitated by the scrum master (the scrum master's role is defined in the next topic). There are also two ancillary roles: stakeholders (customers or vendors) and managers (project or line) who, while not part of the team, will have some interaction with it.

## Product Owner

The product owner's role is to maximise the value of the work of the development team and the products they produce. They are also the 'owner' of the product backlog (requirements). They must have the authority to make all decisions necessary for the development of the products. Their responsibilities include:

- Defining the items in the product backlog and making sure the development team understand them
- Prioritizing and sequencing the items in the product backlog
- Making the product backlog clear and visible to everyone
- Defining what the team will work on next
- Ensuring that the work of the development team delivers value to the products

You can't have responsibility without authority.

## The Development Team

The development team's role is to deliver a potentially releasable increment of the required product at the end of each sprint. They are empowered by the organization to manage and organize their own work, which allows them to optimize their efficiency and effectiveness. The development team will have the following characteristics:

- They must be self-contained and cross-functional in that they possess all the skills and knowledge necessary for the development of the product

- They are self-organized and no one (including the product owner and scrum master) can tell them how to do their work
- While the members of the team may perform many different roles, there are no titles in the team other than Developer
- Individual members of the team may have their own skill sets and areas of focus but overall accountability belongs to the whole team
- The team is not broken down into sub-teams to focus on areas such as design, development or testing
- While not mandatory many teams choose to select or elect a team leader

## Skill Sets

Notwithstanding the above characteristics, the typical skill sets required in the development team are as follows:

- Product Developer: software development or other technical product development skills
- Product Tester: understanding of test procedures, test environments, testing tools or writing test scripts
- Customer: understanding and experience of operating and using the business processes that the new products are designed to support

This is not a definitive list and other specific skills may be needed according to the organization and the project. Team members may have only one or more than one of the required skills but in any event they will decide as a team who to use on what tasks.

## Team Size

The team should be small enough to stay agile and nimble and large enough to get the work done. The typical size of a team is between five and nine people (excluding the product owner and scrum master, unless they are also doing some of the work on the products). Fewer than five people and the team may suffer from a lack of necessary skills while more than nine people and the team becomes too complex and will require a substantial communications overhead.



**Hot tip**

It is essential to identify all the skills required and ensure they are available in the team.

**Beware**

If the team is in danger of becoming too large try to break it down into smaller teams.

# Scrum Master

The Scrum Master's role is to facilitate the team and remove any impediments to their progress in delivering the sprint goal and deliverables. They are not the team leader but act as a buffer between the team and any potentially distracting outside influences. They therefore have a responsibility to help those outside the team understand what is helpful to the team and what is not.

They ensure that the Scrum process and rules are followed as intended and that the team is focused on the tasks in hand. They will also ensure that the team are correctly following the scrum rules and processes.

The Scrum Masters role has been referred to as a servant-leader and in carrying out this role they need to interact with three other elements:

## The Product Owner

The Scrum Master is responsible for providing several services to the product owner:

- Assisting them in finding techniques and methods for effectively managing the product backlog
- Communicating the product owner's vision, goals and the required product backlog items to the development team
- Providing facilitation to the scrum events as needed or requested
- Having a good understanding of and demonstrating agile practices and processes
- Understanding the organization's long-term product requirements and the planning implications of them
- Assisting the team in defining product backlog items

## The Development Team

The Scrum Master is responsible for providing several services to the development team:

- Coaching the team in becoming self-organizing
- Teaching the team to create high-value products

- Dealing with any impediments to the team's progress
- Facilitating scrum events as needed or requested
- Coaching the team where they are not yet fully familiar with the Scrum framework

## The Organization

The Scrum Master is responsible for providing several services to the rest of the organization:

- Coaching the rest of the organization in the adoption of the Scrum framework
- Planning the implementation of Scrum within the organization
- Assisting all the organization's stakeholders in understanding and using Scrum product development methods
- Causing changes to the organization that will increase the scrum team's productivity
- Work with other scrum masters in order to increase the overall effectiveness of the application of Scrum within the organization

## Agile Project Management

Scrum challenges the traditional, command and control, approach to project management. It brings a radically different approach to planning and managing projects and delegates decision making authority to the development team. The use of Scrum makes the development process more effective, reduces faults and ongoing maintenance costs.

## Scrum Events

Part of the Scrum Master's role is to enforce the rules. The scrum events are a critical part of these rules. The sprint event is a container for the other events, while the other events represent formal opportunities to inspect and adapt the products and processes. All these other events have been designed to enable critical transparency and inspection so that a failure to include any of them will increase risk through a reduced transparency and loss of opportunity to inspect and adapt.

Hot tip

As well as being a facilitator, the Scrum Master is also the enforcer of the rules.

# The Sprint

Sprints, which typically last between one week and one month, are the basic unit of development in Scrum. They are timeboxed and produce a usable and potentially releasable product increment.

A sprint consists of a planning meeting, daily scrums, the development work, the sprint review and the sprint retrospective. Each sprint will be used to accomplish something (the sprint goal) and this will be defined and agreed with the product owner in the planning meeting.

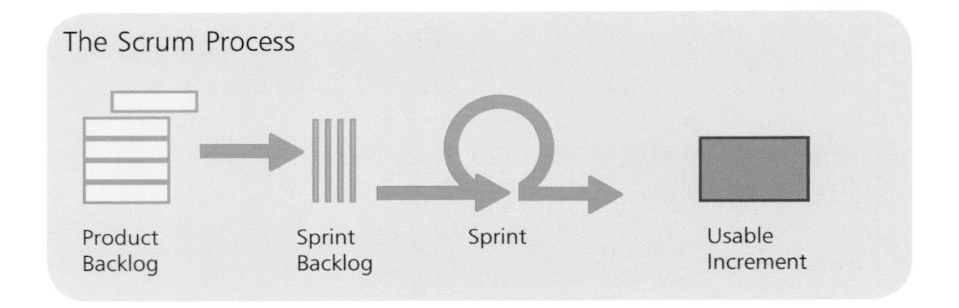


In the sprint planning meeting the product owner informs the team of the items from the product backlog that they wish to be completed in the sprint. The team decides how much of this they can commit to in the sprint and these become the sprint backlog. During the sprint the team develops the items from the sprint backlog into the product. At the end of the sprint a usable product increment exists that is a potential releasable product.

## Sprint Rules

During the course of the sprint the following rules apply:

- No changes can be made that would affect the agreed goal of the sprint
- Once the sprint backlog is agreed it cannot be changed
- The composition of the development team does not get changed
- Quality goals must not be reduced
- But the scope may be clarified and even re-negotiated between the development team and the product owner as more is learned

## Requirements

Once the sprint backlog has been agreed the requirements are frozen for the duration of the sprint. Development is timeboxed so the sprint must end on time. If requirements cannot be completed for any reason they are left out of the product and returned to the product backlog.

Potential changes may come to light during a sprint from the development team, the product owner or the organization. Wherever they may have come from they are held for review and potential inclusion in the next sprint.

If any problems or faults (such as software bugs) come to light during a sprint the development team will try to fix them in the sprint. If they cannot be fixed their resolution will be added to the product backlog for consideration in the next sprint. Sometimes an entire sprint may be dedicated to fixing bugs or other problems with no new functionality being added to the product.

Hot tip

New or changed requirements are added to the product backlog not the sprint backlog.

## Risk Management

By limiting the maximum duration of a sprint to one month, inspection of the product and adaptation of the process has to happen at least once a month. In effect that means that the maximum amount of work that could be wasted is one month's which has the effect of greatly reducing risk to the project.

## Canceling a Sprint

In theory a sprint can be canceled before the end of the timebox if authorized by the product owner. This could happen if the sprint goal becomes obsolete or any further work would be wasted due to other changes in the organization or its business.

If this happens any completed product backlog items are reviewed and if an item is potentially reusable, the product owner would normally accept it. Any incomplete items have a new estimate to completion calculated for them and are put back onto the product backlog.

## Sprint Events

The sprint acts as a type of container for the other sprint events and these are covered in the next few topics of this chapter. Starting with sprint planning, continuing with the daily scrum and ending with the sprint review and sprint retrospective.

# Sprint Planning

At the beginning of each sprint a sprint planning meeting or workshop is held. At the meeting the product owner and the team negotiate what work the team will tackle during the sprint. They then prepare the sprint backlog with estimates of the work effort required to complete each item and identify and communicate how much of the work is likely to be done during the current sprint. This involves the collaborative work of the whole scrum team.

## Meeting Format

The sprint planning meeting is timeboxed to eight hours for a one month sprint and proportionally less for a shorter duration sprint. Whatever the duration the meeting is split into two halves:

- The first half of the meeting involves the product owner and the team and determines what will be included in the product increment to be delivered from the sprint
- The second half of the meeting just involves the team and determines how the work will need to be done in order to deliver the product increment

## The Requirements

The meeting starts with the product owner presenting the product backlog items to the development team. It is up to the product owner to determine which requirements are of the highest priority to the release and which will generate the highest business value. The whole team collaborate on understanding the requirements and what work they will involve, but the team has the power to push back and voice concerns or issues. This is a good thing since the team may be aware of a legitimate impediment keeping the team from moving forward.

The other inputs to the meeting are the latest product increment, the expected capacity of the development team for the duration of the planned sprint and the past performance (velocity) of the team from previous sprints.

Based on these inputs the development team then assesses how many of the items from the product backlog they believe they will be able to complete in the sprint. This then becomes part of the sprint goal, which is the objective for implementing the product backlog items together with guidance for the development team.

### The Plan

In the second half of the meeting the product owner is typically asked to leave while the development team works out how it will build the required functionality into the product increments for this sprint. While the product owner is asked to leave so that the team can candidly discuss the work, they are still expected to be available to answer questions, clarify acceptance criteria, or renegotiate. The product backlog items together with the plan for delivering them becomes the sprint backlog.

The team will normally start by designing the enhanced product and identifying the work that will be needed to turn it into a working product increment. This work then needs to be estimated so that the team can forecast how much of the requirements from the product backlog they will be able to deliver in the sprint.

The first few days work of the sprint is broken down into tasks or units of one day or less for the first few daily scrums. The remainder will be on-going through the sprint.

### Work Allocation

The development team then organizes who will do what by allocating the tasks to the team members. If the team then comes to the conclusion that it has too much or too little work for the sprint it will need to re-negotiate the sprint backlog items to be included with the product owner.

By the end of the meeting the development team should be in a position to explain to the product owner and scrum master how they intended to work to achieve the sprint goal and deliver the product increment.

### Sprint Goal

The sprint goal should give the development team some flexibility in the functionality that will be delivered in the increment. This is normally achieved through the prioritization of requirements. Once the sprint goals are defined and agreed, the development team is ready to get to work.

As the team works on the development of the product it keeps the sprint goal firmly in mind. If they uncover any problems or issues as the functionality is implemented they may need to go back and re-negotiate the scope of the sprint backlog.

# Daily Scrum

Hot tip 

Ideally the meetings should take place in the development team's work place.

Each day during the sprint the development team hold a meeting referred to as the daily scrum or daily stand-up (as it is usually held standing up). The meeting has very specific rules:

- The meeting starts precisely on time
- All are welcome but only the development team speak
- The meeting is timeboxed at 15 minutes
- The meeting should take place in the same location and at the same time every day

During the meeting each team member answers three questions:

1. What have you done since yesterday?
2. What are you planning to do today?
3. What impediments or obstacles have you encountered?

## The Meeting

It is the scrum master's role to ensure that the development team hold the daily scrum, but it is the development team's responsibility to run it. The scrum master will also facilitate the time keeping so that it keeps within the 15 minute limit.

The scrum master will also enforce the rule that only the development team speak during the meeting. The meeting is for their benefit, anyone else is just there to observe and learn.

Daily scrums result in improved communications and remove the need for other meetings. They identify and deal with obstacles to development, promote speedy decision making and increase the development team's product knowledge. It is a key inspect and adapt meeting.

Hot tip 

A template for a daily scrum is provided for your use on our website. Go to www.ineasysteps.com/resource-centre/downloads

## Progress Tracking

The daily scrum helps the development team to assess their progress towards the sprint goal and, by projecting it forward, how they are doing towards completing the work in the sprint backlog. The daily scrum improves the probability that the development team will meet the sprint goal.

# Sprint Review

A Sprint Review is held at the end of each sprint to inspect the increment and make any required changes to the product backlog. It should be an informal meeting to allow the increment to be presented or demonstrated and feedback to be obtained. It should also foster collaboration between the scrum team and the other stakeholders on what was done during the sprint.

Based on the presentation, inspection and any changes to the product backlog the participants then collaborate on what could be done next.

The meeting will be timeboxed to four hours for a one month sprint and proportionally less for a shorter sprint.

## The Review Meeting

The sprint review meeting should be carried out through the following five steps:

1. The product owner identifies what has been done and what has not been done from the sprint backlog

2. The development team discuss what went well during the sprint, what problems or issues they encountered and how they resolved them

3. The development team then demonstrate the work that it has done and answers any questions about it and the increment developed

4. The product owner then discusses the product backlog as it now stands and projects forward to the likely completion date based on progress to date

5. Finally the whole group collaborate on what to do next so that the sprint review provides helpful input to the next sprint planning meeting

The result of the sprint review is a revised product backlog that defines the probable product backlog items for the next sprint. It may also be revised to incorporate any new opportunities that have been identified.

# Sprint Retrospective

The Sprint Retrospective gives the scrum team the opportunity to inspect itself and the way it is working, identify any improvements that could be made and create a plan for introducing them during the next sprint. The two main questions the team should ask itself are: What went well during the sprint? And what could be improved in the next sprint?

The meeting should take place after the sprint review and before the next sprint planning meeting. It should be a three hour timeboxed meeting for a one month sprint, proportionally less for a shorter sprint.

The meeting has three objectives:

1. To inspect how the sprint went with regard to the people, relationships, processes and tools used
2. To identify and sequence the things that went well and the potential improvements that could be made
3. To develop a plan for implementing these identified improvements to the way the scrum team will work in future

## The Meeting

During the meeting the scrum master should encourage the team to focus on improvements they can make within the scrum process framework and their development processes and practices. The goal should be to make it more effective and enjoyable for the next sprint. The scrum team should also look for ways of improving the product quality by adapting the agreed definition of 'done' as necessary.

## Inspect and Adapt

By the end of the meeting the scrum team should have identified the improvements that it will be implementing in the next sprint. This is the adaptation of the results of their own self inspection.

While it is possible to implement improvements at any time, the sprint retrospective provides a formal opportunity for the scrum team to focus on inspection and adaptation of its tools, processes, interactions and methods.

Hot tip

By having a regular but not too frequent review the team will keep improving its working.

# Scrum Artifacts

The Scrum Artifacts are the things that represent work or value in such a way as to provide transparency together with opportunities for inspection and adaptation. The artifacts defined by Scrum are designed to maximize the transparency of key information to enable the scrum team to deliver a successful increment. The Scrum Artifacts are the product backlog, the sprint backlog and the burndown charts.

## Product Backlog

The product backlog is a high-level list that is maintained throughout the entire project. It contains a broad description of all the potential features, prioritized by business value. It is the list of what will be developed in order of importance. It should contain rough estimates of the business value and estimates of the likely development work effort.

Hot tip

The product backlog is sometimes called the prioritized requirements list or features backlog.

The product owner can use these development estimates to produce a possible timeline and also to assist in the prioritization process. For example, if two requirements have the same estimate of development work the one with the greater business value can be prioritized higher. The product backlog and business value of each item are the product owners while the development work effort estimates are set by the development team.

## Sprint Backlog

The sprint backlog is the list of work that the development team will address during the sprint. Each feature is broken down into tasks, which should normally be between four and sixteen hours work. With this level of detail the whole team can understand what needs to be done and pick a task from the list. The tasks on the sprint backlog are not assigned but are picked up by team members as needed, according to priority and the skills of the particular team member.

## Burndown Charts

The sprint burndown chart will normally be publicly displayed in the development team's work area and illustrates the amount of work remaining in the sprint backlog. It will be updated daily to reflect progress.

Don't forget

Burndown charts are an excellent way of communicating project progress.

In addition to the sprint burndown chart there will usually be a higher level burndown chart for the product release and a top-level burndown chart for the entire project.

# Product Backlog

Don't forget

The Product Backlog can also be called the Prioritized Requirements List.

Hot tip

A template for a product backlog is provided for your use on our website. Go to www.ineasysteps.com/resource-centre/downloads

The product backlog is a sequenced list of the requirements for changes to the product. It should contain everything that might be needed in the product and is the only source of requirements. The product owner is responsible for the product backlog, its content, sequencing and availability.

The product backlog is a dynamic and evolving object. At the start of the project it is a high-level list of the identified requirements at that stage. As the project progresses it will evolve as the product evolves. It will continually change as people identify what the product needs to be competitive, appropriate and useful.

## Content

It will contain all the required features, functions, enhancements and fixes that may result in changes to the product in future releases. For each item it will record a description, the value to the business, any associated risks, the priority and an estimate of the work effort required to produce it. It will be sequenced in order of importance, the higher it is the more important it is for the business to implement it.

## Refinement

The product backlog is progressively refined in that items with the highest priority are more detailed while the lower priority items are more coarse-grained. As items are more clearly defined the estimates for their development become more accurate. The items that have been selected for the next sprint are the most detailed and they will have been decomposed to the most detailed level so that they can be developed within one sprint. These items are then ready for selection in the next sprint planning meeting.

## Continued Evolution

As the product is used and the business or marketplace provides feedback on it, the product backlog will become larger. Requirements will never stop changing in response to business needs or market conditions so the product backlog continues to evolve as long as the product exists.

## Backlog Grooming

Product backlog grooming is the ongoing process where the product owner and the development team collaborate on the details of the product backlog, adding detail, updating estimates and re-sequencing the items.

# Sprint Backlog

The sprint backlog is the set of product backlog items that have been selected for the sprint, together with a plan for how they will be developed for the product increment to meet the sprint goal. It is the development team's forecast of the functionality that they will be building into the next increment together with the work effort needed to deliver it. Each item is broken down into tasks, which should ideally require no more than one day's work.

The sprint backlog is another excellent way of communicating project progress.

## Done Items

The sprint backlog defines the work that the development team will need to perform to turn product backlog items into 'done' features. When all the features that can be done have been done, the increment is deemed to have been done.

## Definition of Done

When a product backlog item or an increment is deemed to have been done the whole scrum team must agree that it has been done and what 'done' means to the team to ensure transparency. Part of the definition of done will be that the feature or increment is usable as the product owner may choose to release any increment if it would be beneficial. Every increment adds to previous increments and is tested thoroughly to ensure that all the features work together. Finally it should be noted that as the scrum team develops they should expand their definition of done to include more stringent quality criteria.

## Changing the Sprint Backlog

The sprint backlog should have sufficient detail in the plan to allow progress to be monitored against it in the daily scrum. The development team will develop and modify the sprint backlog during the sprint as they work through the details and discover more about the work they will have to complete to achieve the sprint goal.

As new work is identified the development team add it to the sprint backlog. As work is completed the estimated work to completion is updated to reflect what still has to be done. If any elements of the plan are found to be unnecessary they are removed. All of this is under the control of the development team during the sprint.

The sprint backlog remains a visible picture of the work that the development team plans to complete during the sprint.

A template for a sprint backlog is provided for your use on our website. Go to www.ineasysteps.com/resource-centre/downloads

# Progress Monitoring

During a sprint the amount of work to complete each task (the estimate to completion) is updated each day for the daily scrum until a task is completed. So at any point during the sprint the total work remaining to reach the sprint goal can be summed up from the remaining tasks. The development team can then use this projected forward to manage their progress and forecast the likelihood of their achieving the sprint goal.

## Burndown Charts

A burndown chart is a graphical representation of the amount of work left to do against time. The outstanding work (the sprint backlog) is usually illustrated on the vertical axis and time on the horizontal. The following is a typical sprint burndown chart:

Hot tip

A template for a burndown chart is provided for your use on our website. Go to www.ineasysteps.com/resource-centre/downloads

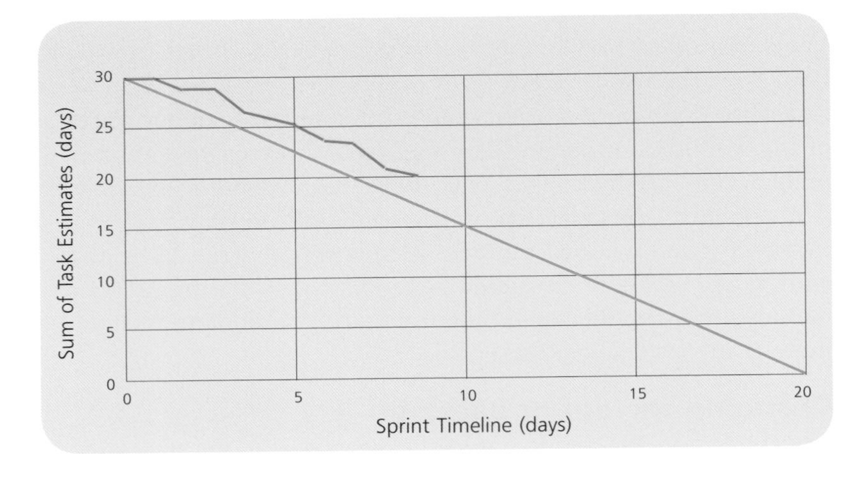


The chart above may indicate that the work was initially underestimated or that no allowance was made for the team getting up to speed. The development team can use this information to decide if they can still achieve the sprint goal or if they need to remove some items from the sprint backlog.

## Velocity

Velocity is the measure of the development team's delivery capacity in a timebox.  The unit of measure is the same as that used for estimating which is most often days work. The predicted velocity at the start of the project is guessed or based on data from previous projects. After that the actual velocity is measured at the end of each sprint.

To do this the estimates for the features done in the sprint are totaled. This gives the actual velocity for the sprint, which is then used to predict the velocity for subsequent sprints.

It should become apparent after only a couple of sprints if the development team has sufficient capacity to deliver the features and achieve the sprint goal. If it looks like the team won't be able to deliver then corrective action can be taken by cutting scope. This will result in a sustainable pace that the team should be able to maintain.

Velocity helps the team to make more accurate estimates in future.

## Hit Rate

The hit rate is the percentage of work allocated to the sprint that was actually completed. Ideally the team should have a hit rate near 100%. A low hit rate indicates the team is struggling to meet their commitments which will need to be investigated as it might be caused by over commitment or some other obstacle.

## Work Remaining

Each day the team estimates the work remaining on each active task. The estimate of work remaining will hopefully go down over time, but it may rise if the task is more complicated than was originally anticipated.

## Project Cost

In most organizations the cost of a project must be tracked to ensure it does not go over budget. If it is being tracked it can be reported on.

## Information Radiators

Their purpose is to radiate information via big visible charts to create an informative workspace. The team just has to glance at them to know how they're doing. Similarly (informed) visitors only need to walk into the team area and look round for about 15 seconds to know what is going on. Obviously these charts are indicative and a longer investigation would be needed to delve into any issues.

Hot tip

Information radiators are another excellent form of communicating project progress.

## Project Progress

By tracking the amount of work remaining from each sprint review and comparing this to the previous sprint reviews, progress towards the completed iteration can be tracked. Likewise progress towards the complete project can be tracked.

# Summary

- Scrum provides a framework (the team, events, artifacts and the rules) within which people can address complex problems
- Scrum theory is based on experiential learning theory that goes through a cycle of planning, executing, reviewing and concluding
- The scrum team consists of the product owner, the development team and the scrum master
- The optimum size for the development team is between five and nine people (not counting the product owner and scrum master)
- The scrum master's role is to facilitate the team's processes, deal with any obstructions and ensure the correct processes are being followed
- Sprints, typically lasting a month, start with a planning meeting, followed by daily scrums and a review and retrospective
- Sprint planning takes place in a timeboxed meeting in which the product owner and team agree which items will be included and how they will carry out the work
- The daily scrum lasts 15 minutes and each team member says what they did yesterday, what they will do today and any problems they have encountered
- The sprint review inspects the increment produced by the sprint and agrees any changes required to the product backlog
- The sprint retrospective gives the team the chance to look back at the sprint and develop a plan for implementing any improvements
- The product backlog is the sequenced list of all known requirements for the product
- The sprint backlog is the work to be carried out in the sprint and the plan for how it will be done
- Progress monitoring is through estimating the work still to be done and plotting this against the planned velocity

# 5 Extreme Programming

*Extreme Programming is one of several popular agile processes. It has a focus on customer satisfaction and rapid delivery of product when it is needed.*

# Background

Extreme Programming (XP) or eXtreme Programming as it is sometimes written to fit the XP acronym is a software development methodology. The first recorded use of the technique was by Kent Beck on the Chrysler Comprehensive Compensation (C3) payroll system in 1996 but the technique has been used subsequently at many other organizations large and small. The reason the name was chosen was to reflect the fact that it is said to take best practices to extreme levels.

## Customer Satisfaction

One reason for its popularity is the focus on customer satisfaction that it brings. Rather than delivering everything the customer wants at some future date it aims to deliver what the customer wants as they need it. The method uses frequent releases in short development timeboxes together with formal checkpoints where new and changed customer requirements can be incorporated.

As this is very much in line with the Scrum philosophy it will come as no surprise that extreme programming works well and is often used inside the Scrum framework.



## Planning/Feedback Loops

The diagram at the top of the page opposite illustrates the planning and feedback loops built into the method. It also includes an indication of the timescale or frequency of the loops.

In XP the requirements are defined through user stories written on cards. These define the scope of the project and are also used to create the plans.

## Release Plan

The release plan looks several months into the future and will include all the user stories that represent the functionality the customer wants in the release.

In Scrum the Release Plan is the Product Backlog and the Iteration Plan is the Sprint Backlog.

## Iteration Plan

The plan for the next iteration then includes as many of the customer's priority user stories as the team believe they can build in the iteration timebox. This will typically be from one to four weeks.

Finally the user stories will be broken down into the tasks that will be required to incorporate them into the product. Members

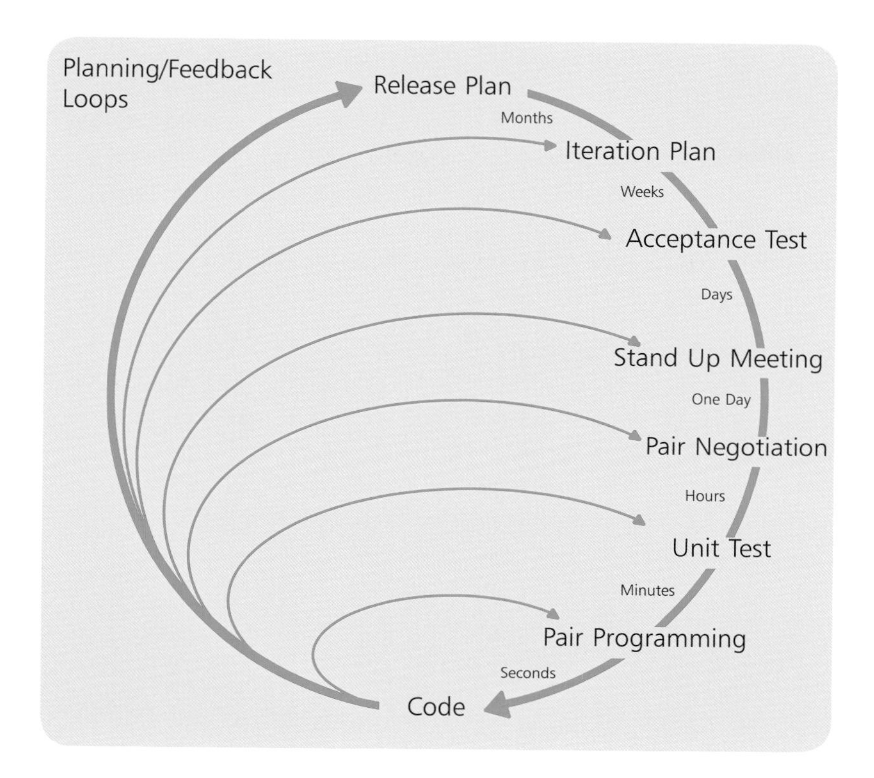


of the development team then select which tasks they will work on. A basic tenet of extreme programming is that the developers are responsible for proving that their code works correctly to the customer so the acceptance tests are designed ahead of the coding.

## Pair Programming

In extreme programming all production code is developed using pair programming and unit testing is used to test every piece of code developed. The feedback loops illustrated above show that there is continual feedback from the coding process, as the code is developed and tested, to the unit test cases and to who is doing what in the pair of programmers.

## Daily Stand-Up

At the daily stand-up meeting the programmers give feedback on their progress, plan for the coming day and any issues they have encountered. Feedback on the acceptance tests and iteration plan is through the customers to the development team who will use the results of the coding and testing to refine their requirements.

The daily stand-up meeting is common to all the agile methodologies. A template for a daily stand-up is provided for your use on our website. Go to www.ineasysteps.com/resource-centre/downloads

# Concept

The major concept behind extreme programming is that the method, if correctly implemented, will result in an improved quality product, customer satisfaction and improved productivity. Extreme programming assumes that the customer will change their mind and there will be other changes of requirements through the coding and testing of the product. It empowers the developers to respond to changes even late in the project.

Extreme programming tries to mitigate for this through multiple short development iterations. Changes are regarded as a natural and desirable aspect of a software development project and should therefore be planned for in place of trying to define a firm set of requirements.

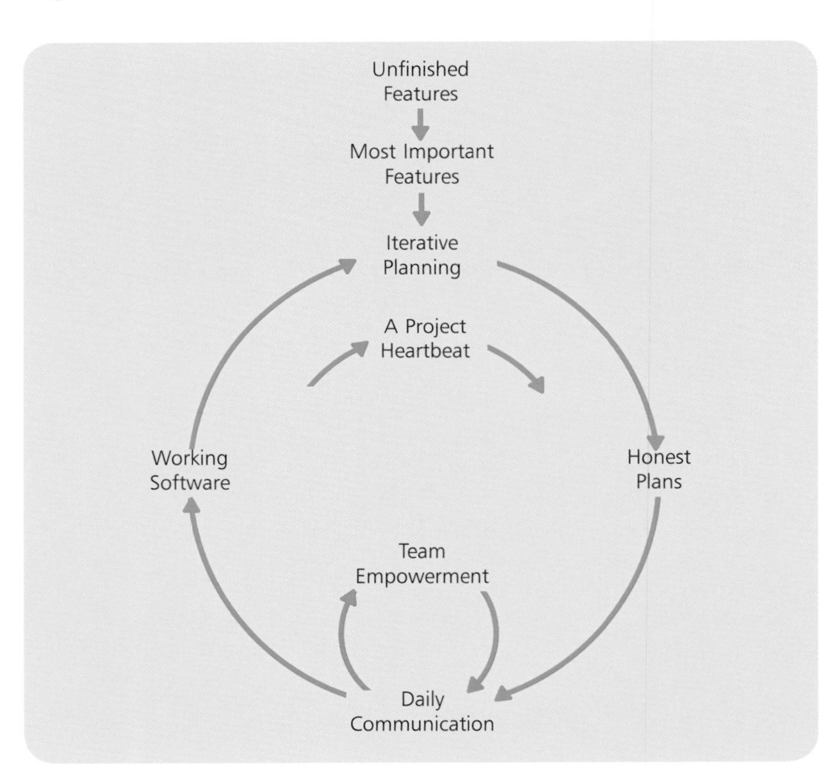

A Project Heartbeat refers to one iteration of the product.

The diagram above illustrates the concept of the process with each iteration starting by selecting a workable quantity of the most important features. The iteration is then planned (with honesty) and the development team are empowered to develop and test the software with the customer to produce working software.

Extreme programming puts a heavy emphasis on teamwork with the developers, customers and managers all being equal partners in a collaborative team. The developers communicate continually with one another and with the customer. They keep their design simple and get continuing feedback by testing right from the start. They deliver the product to the customer as early as possible and implement changes as they are suggested.

Extreme programming has a simple set of rules (set out later in this chapter) and defines four basic development activities: coding, testing, listening and designing.

## Coding

The main product of the system development process is working code. Without this there is no product. But code can also help to identify the best solution to a requirement by illustrating options and prototypes. Code can even be used to illustrate a problem which is difficult to explain.

## Testing

Unit testing will prove whether or not any feature works as intended. The programmers develop as many automated test cases that might break the code as they can. Each piece of code is tested before they move onto the next feature. Only when all tests have been run successfully is the code considered to be complete.

Acceptance testing is used by the customer to verify that the code as built and unit tested meets their actual requirements. The acceptance test cases are developed in the exploration phase of release planning corroboratively by the customer and developers.

## Listening

The programmers must listen to and understand what the customer needs the product to do. This means they need to understand the business logic behind the requirements so that they can give the customer feedback on how the requirement can be met or if it cannot be met. Communication is facilitated by co-locating the customer with the developers.

## Design

Good design is critical to building a successful product. In extreme programming the design should be as simple as possible to reduce complexity and minimize inter-dependencies.

**Don't forget**

Close customer or business collaboration is a feature of all agile methodologies.

# Values

In "Extreme Programming Explained", Kent Beck defines five values: communication, simplicity, feedback, courage and respect.

## Communication

Building software systems starts with the need for the customer to communicate their requirements to the developers. In traditional software development methodologies this task was achieved by requirements documentation. Extreme programming techniques are methods for rapidly building and communicating business knowledge and understanding among the development team members. The goal is to give the developers the same view of the required system as that held by the users of the system. To achieve this, extreme programming favors simple designs, common metaphors, collaboration between users and programmers, frequent verbal communication and feedback.

## Simplicity

Extreme programming encourages starting out with the simplest solution. Extra functionality can then be added to it through the life of the product. The difference between this and the traditional system development methods is the focus on designing and coding for the needs of today instead of trying to define everything up front. The downside of this is it can sometimes require more work to change the system later. Supporters of XP, however, claim that this is more than compensated for by the advantage of not investing in possible future requirements that might change before they become relevant. Designing and coding for uncertain future requirements can risk spending resources on something that might not be needed. Simplicity in design and coding should improve the quality of communication. A simple design with simple code should be readily understood by all the programmers in the team.

Good design is simple design, so keep it simple.

## Feedback

In extreme programming, feedback can come from the programmers, the customer, the team or the system itself:

- By writing and running unit and integration tests, the programmers receive direct feedback from the state of the system after implementing any changes
- The acceptance tests are written by the customer and the testers, who will both receive feedback about the current state

of the system. As this review is planned once every two or three weeks the customer receives feedback and can easily steer the development

- When customers come up with new requirements in the planning process, the team directly give an estimation of the time that it will take to implement them, providing immediate feedback
- Any flaws in the system are easily illustrated by writing a unit test that proves the code will break. Direct feedback from the system tells the programmers to re-code it

## Courage

Several of the practices used in extreme programming embody courage. The first is to design and code for today and not for tomorrow. This is to avoid getting bogged down in design and expending a lot of effort in trying to implement things that may not eventually be required. Courage enables developers to feel comfortable with refactoring their code when necessary. This means reviewing the existing system and modifying it so that future changes can be implemented more easily.

Another example of courage is knowing when to get rid of source code that is obsolete, regardless of how much effort was originally used to create that code. Courage can also mean persistence: if a programmer gets stuck on a complex problem for some time, by staying persistent they should eventually solve it.

## Respect

In extreme programming, everyone should show respect for others and also have self-respect. Programmers should never commit changes that break compilation, make existing unit-tests fail, or otherwise delay the work of their colleagues. Team members respect their own work by striving for high quality and the best design for the solution at hand through refactoring.

Adopting the four earlier values leads to respect from the other members of the team. Nobody in the team should feel unappreciated or ignored. This ensures a high level of motivation and encourages loyalty toward the team and toward the goal of the project. This value is dependent upon the other values, and is very much oriented toward people in a team.

Hot tip

When the team agrees to these values they will be a great team.

# Rules

The 29 rules of extreme programming are quite simple. They are published on the XP website (www.extremeprogramming.org), broken down into the following five categories:

Don't forget

User Stories were introduced on page 88.

## Planning

User stories are written by the customer to represent their requirements and used by developers to estimate the work.

Release planning involves turning the user stories and the associated work estimates into the release schedule.

Make frequent small releases by producing working software every one or two weeks. The customer decides which will be released.

Hot tip

A template for user stories is provided for your use on our website. Go to www.ineasysteps.com/resource-centre/downloads

Divide the project into short iterations which are kept constant through the project. This assists velocity tracking and control.

Each iteration begins with iteration planning which turns the user stories into a list of tasks for the developers.



## Managing

Give the team a dedicated, open work space. This will aid communication and encourage people to work together.

Set a sustainable pace by using the project velocity to make future estimates and schedules more accurate.

Start each day with a stand-up meeting in the team's open work space. This gives every member of the team the chance to communicate.

Measure the project velocity at the end of each iteration by adding up the amount of work in the completed user stories.

Move people around within the team to spread knowledge and provide cross-training of skills.

When XP breaks, fix it. Follow the rules to start with but be prepared to change the process if the team decides to do so.

## Designing

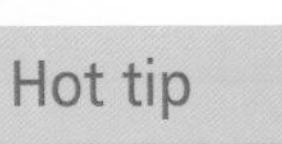

Hot tip

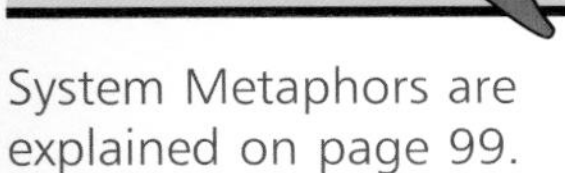

System Metaphors are explained on page 99.

Simplicity: a simple design is always faster and easier to implement than a complex one.

Choose a system metaphor. It is much easier to explain the project using a metaphor than to produce a vast document.

Use CRC (Class, Responsibilities and Collaboration) cards for design sessions. These represent the objects in the system.

Create spike solutions to reduce risk in dealing with problems. Spike solutions are throw-away code to explore options.

No functionality is added early. Never build anything into the system before it is needed.

Refactor whenever and wherever possible by removing unwanted code. In the long run this will save time and money.

Make the customer a full part of the team from the outset.

## Coding

The customer is always available. They are not only there to help the development team but to be part of it.

Code must be written to agreed standards. This will improve quality and aid refactoring.

Code the unit test first. This will help the programmer understand the requirement and develop the code.

All production code is pair programmed. Two people working at one computer will produce better code more quickly.

Only one pair integrates code at a time. If parallel integration takes place new code will not have been tested fully.

Integrate often. Every few hours at the very least.

Set up a dedicated integration computer. This controls the integration process and prevents parallel integration

Use collective ownership. It encourages everyone to contribute.

## Testing

All code must be unit tested, using a unit test framework and by setting up the tests before developing the code.

All code must pass all unit tests before it can be released.

When a bug is found tests are created to guard against it coming back.

Acceptance tests (preferably automated) are run often and the scores are published.

# Principles

The principles that underlie extreme programming are based on the values described earlier in this chapter. They are intended to foster decision making in an extreme programming development project. The principles are intended to be more concrete than the values and more easily translated to guidance in a practical, work place environment.

## Feedback

In extreme programming, feedback is most useful if it happens rapidly. It states that the time between taking an action and its feedback is critical to learning and making changes. Contact with the customer occurs more often than in traditional system development methods, due to the frequency of the iterations. This gives the customer a clear insight into the system being developed so that they can give feedback and steer the development.

Unit tests also contribute to the rapid feedback principle. When writing code, the unit test provides direct feedback to the programmer about how the system reacts to the changes made. If the changes being made also affect another part of the system that is not in the scope of the programmer making them, they may not be aware of introducing a flaw. Integration testing or acceptance testing should then provide feedback on this problem.

## Assuming Simplicity

In traditional system development methodology the approach is to plan for the future and code for reusability. The extreme programming approach rejects these ideas and states that making big changes all at once does not work.

The extreme programming approach is about treating every problem as if its solution was extremely simple. Changes are applied incrementally through small releases every few weeks. When many little steps are being taken, the customer also has frequent visibility and more control over the development process and the system being developed.

## Embracing Change

The principle of embracing change is about expecting it and welcoming it rather than rejecting it. If it appears that the customer's requirements have changed dramatically, the programmers will just take this on board and plan the new requirements for the next iteration of the product.

# Scalability

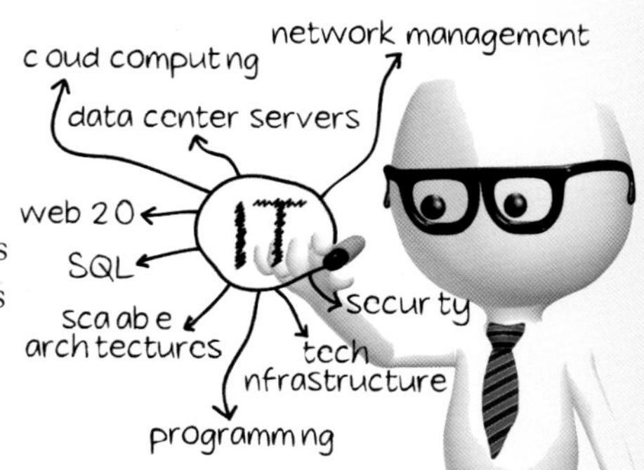


Although extreme programming has been proved to work well with development teams as small as two people it only really scales up to teams of around twelve people. Above this number the team will start to fragment and communications will demand a higher overhead.

## Work Around

Various potential ways of getting around this limitation have been explored. One way is to break a project up into smaller subsets and the project team into smaller sub-teams. Claims have been made that this process has been used successfully on teams of over a hundred developers but this has not been substantiated. Industrial Extreme Programming was introduced as an evolution of extreme programming, it is intended to work with large and distributed teams. But again this has not yet been substantiated through use.

## When to Use XP

First and foremost extreme programming was designed to be used where requirements will change and develop throughout the project. If a project fits this model then extreme programming is likely to be more successful than a traditional approach.

Extreme programming reduces the risk of a project being late by its concentration on fixed delivery dates. So if a project has a critical delivery date, extreme programming is more likely to meet it than a traditional approach.

Extreme programming works best with small teams and does not scale up well. However, if a project has dynamic requirements and a critical delivery date, a smaller team may well be more effective than a large team. With extreme programming, most organizations also report greater programmer productivity.

Extreme programming uses an extended development team that includes customers and managers as well as programmers. If a project can benefit from a heavy customer involvement in defining requirements and testing the developed product then extreme programming is likely to be the best option.

In summary, on a time-critical project where requirements are fluid and you can deploy a small team of programmers and customers then use extreme programming.

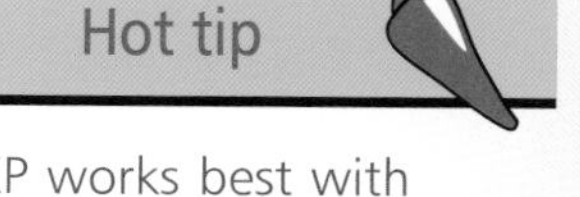


XP works best with small, multi-functional teams and short project timescales.

# Practices

Extreme programming is said to have 12 practices, grouped into four areas:

## Fine Scale Feedback

Pair Programming: means that all code is produced by two people working on one task on one workstation. One programmer has control over the workstation and is thinking mostly about the coding in detail. The other programmer is focused on the big picture and continually reviews the code being produced by the first programmer. Programmers should swap roles regularly.

Planning Game: The main planning process is called the planning game. The game is a meeting that occurs once per iteration and is divided into two parts: release planning and iteration planning.

Test-driven Development: Unit testing uses automated tests of the functionality of pieces of the code. They are written before the code is started and this is intended to stimulate the programmer to think about conditions in their code that could fail. The programmer is finished with any piece of code when they cannot think of any further condition on which the code might fail.

Always include the customer or business end user in the team.

Whole Team: The customer is not the person who pays the bill, but the one who will really use the system. They should be on hand and available for questions at all times. For instance, the team developing a financial administration system should include a financial administrator.

## Continuous Process

Continuous Integration: The development team should always be working on the latest version of the software. Since different team members may have versions saved locally with various changes and improvements, they should upload their current version to the code repository every few hours, or when a significant break presents itself. Continuous integration will avoid delays later on in the project cycle, caused by integration problems.

Refactoring (Design Improvement): XP doctrine advocates programming only what is needed today and implementing it as simply as possible. This may result in changes in one part of the code affecting lots of other parts of the code. If this occurs, the system is telling you to refactor your code by changing the architecture, making it simpler and more generic.

Small Releases: The delivery of the software is done via frequent releases of live functionality adding value. The small releases help the customer to gain confidence in the progress of the project. This helps maintain the concept of the whole team as the customer can now come up with suggestions on the project based on real experience.

## Shared Understanding

Coding Standards: These are a set of rules that the development team agree to adhere to. The standard specifies a consistent style and format for source code, within the chosen programming language, as well as various programming constructs and patterns that should be avoided to reduce the probability of defects. The coding standard may be a standard convention specified by the language or one defined by the team.

Collective Code Ownership: This means that everyone is jointly responsible for all the code. This in turn means that everybody is allowed to change any part of the code. Pair programming contributes to this practice: by working in different pairs, all the programmers get to see all the parts of the code. If an error occurs in the code any programmer may fix it.

Simple Design: Whenever a new piece of code is written, the author should ask themselves 'is there a simpler way to introduce the same functionality?'. If the answer is yes, the simpler course should be chosen. Refactoring should also be used, to make complex code more simple.

System Metaphor: This is a story that everyone can use to describe how the system works. It's also a naming concept for classes and methods that makes it easy for a team member to guess the functionality of a particular class/method from its name.

## Programmer Welfare

Sustainable Pace: Software developers should not work more than 40 hour weeks and, if there is overtime one week, then the next week should not include more overtime. Since the development cycles are short cycles of continuous integration and full release cycles are more frequent, projects do not follow the typical build up of pressure (requiring increasing overtime) towards the end of the project. Also included in this concept is the idea that people perform best and most creatively if they are rested.

Beware 

If you overwork the team for sustained periods the quality of their work will deteriorate.

# Issues

There has been much debate on the principles, practices and rules in extreme programming. The major issues and potentially controversial aspects of extreme programming that have been identified are as follows:

## Change Control

Proponents of extreme programming claim that, by having the customer co-located with the developers, change requests are handled informally, the process is flexible and it saves the cost of formal overhead. Critics claim this can lead to costly rework and project scope creep beyond what was agreed or funded.

Change control boards are a sign that there are potential conflicts in project objectives and constraints between different users. Extreme programming methodology depends on the development team being able to assume a unified client viewpoint. The programmer can then concentrate on coding rather than documentation of compromise objectives and constraints.

## Requirements

Requirements are defined incrementally rather than by trying to get them all agreed in advance. Requirements are also expressed as automated acceptance tests rather than specification documents. Critics claim that this is imprecise and may lead to requirements being missed.

## Design

There is no big design exercise up front. Most of the design activity takes place on the fly and incrementally, starting with the simplest solution that could possibly work and adding complexity only when it's required by failing tests or added functionality. Critics compare this to debugging a system into appearance. They claim it will result in more re-design effort than would have been required to design the whole system at the start.

## Customer Representative

As a customer representative is embedded with the development team this role can become a single point of failure for the project if they get the requirements wrong. Some customer representatives have also found it to be a source of stress. Critics claim that there is a further potential danger of a non-technical person micro-managing the developers by trying to dictate the use of technical software features and architecture.

## Dependence on XP

As extreme programming cannot be implemented piece meal, there is a dependence upon all of the aspects of XP. It has been likened by some critics to "a ring of poisonous snakes, daisy-chained together. All it takes is for one of them to wriggle loose, and you've got a very angry, poisonous snake heading your way."

## XP Methods

Extreme programming's initial buzz and controversial tenets, such as pair programming and continuous design, have attracted much criticism. However, agile practitioners believe this to be due to the critics misunderstanding of agile development.

## Other Criticisms

Many other criticisms have been levelled against extreme programming, including the following:

- A methodology is only as effective as the people involved and extreme programming does not solve this
- It can be used as a means of bleeding money from customers through lack of defining a deliverable
- It only works with senior-level developers
- Requires frequent meetings at enormous expense to customers
- Requires too much cultural change to adopt
- Can lead to more difficult contractual negotiations
- Can be very inefficient if the requirements for one area of code keep changing through various iterations
- Impossible to develop realistic estimates of work effort to provide a quote, because no one knows the entire scope
- Can increase the risk of scope creep due to the lack of detailed requirements documentation
- Agile is feature driven and non-functional quality attributes are hard to define as user stories

Proponents say that these can all be managed in an agile project environment but they do underline the need for the organization to embrace the methodology fully.

Beware

XP must be implemented completely or it will not work.

# Summary

- Extreme Programming (XP) is based on taking the best software development practices to extreme levels
- Rather than delivering everything the customer wants at some future date, it aims to deliver what the customer needs, when they need it
- Requirements are defined as user stories, written on cards, that are used to drive the plan and acceptance testing
- XP uses planning and feedback loops so that feedback is received at every level and acted on immediately
- Pair programming, unit testing and the daily stand-up meetings all provide immediate feedback
- The method, when correctly implemented, will result in improved product quality, customer satisfaction and improved productivity
- It defines four basic development activities: coding, testing, listening and design
- It is based on five values: communication, simplicity, feedback, courage and respect
- There are 29 rules of XP, covering planning, managing, designing, coding and testing
- The principles that form the basis of XP are feedback, assuming simplicity and embracing change
- While XP is not currently suitable for a very large development team, it is the best approach for a smaller project, with loosely defined requirements, a critical timeframe and heavy customer involvement
- It is said to have twelve practices grouped into four areas: fine scale feedback, continuous process, shared understanding and programmer welfare
- Some issues and criticisms have been levelled at XP such as poor change control, requirements definition and design but these can all be managed as long as the organization fully embraces the methodology

# 6 Lean Development

*Lean Development is an agile methodology that is based on the elimination of waste. It has been developed from the very effective Toyota Production System.*

# Concepts

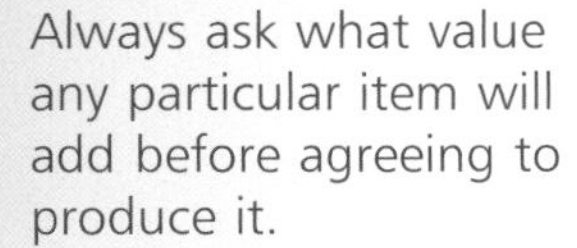


Always ask what value any particular item will add before agreeing to produce it.

Lean software development has evolved from the lean production processes in the automotive industry. A lean process is one that considers the expenditure of resources for any goal, other than the creation of value for the end customer, to be wasteful and therefore a target for elimination. Value is defined as any function or process that a customer would be willing to pay for.

## Philosophy

Lean manufacturing is a management philosophy best exemplified by the Toyota Production System (TPS). Toyota's growth, from a small company to the world's largest automobile manufacturer, has illustrated the benefits that can be achieved.

Toyota defined three broad types of waste: muda (waste), mura (unevenness) and muri (unreasonable work imposed by management). Muri focuses on planning the process and on what work can be avoided through design. Mura then focuses on how the work design is implemented and the elimination of fluctuations in volume or quality. Muda is then identified after the process is in operation through fluctuations in output.

## The Seven Muda

TPS also identified the seven areas of waste to be eliminated in order to improve overall customer value:

- Transport: Having to move things that are not actually required out of the way so as to perform the processing
- Inventory: Raw materials, work in progress and finished products that are no longer being processed
- Motion: People, material or equipment having to move or walk more than is required to perform the processing
- Waiting: Idle time while waiting for some other production process to be completed
- Overproduction: Producing something before it is actually needed (production ahead of demand)
- Over Processing: Additional activity required due to poor design or poor tools
- Defects: The effort involved in inspecting for defects and then fixing them

## Fourteen Principles

Craig Larman and Bas Vodde in their Lean Primer focus on the concept of lean thinking and summarize Toyota's philosophy as a set of 14 principles. These are as valid for software development as for manufacturing processes:

- Base management decisions on a long-term philosophy, if necessary at the expense of short-term financial goals
- Move toward flow, move to ever-smaller batch sizes and cycle times so as to deliver value fast and expose weaknesses
- Use pull (demand) systems and decide as late as possible
- Level the work to reduce variability and overburdening so as to remove unevenness in the process
- Build a culture of stopping and fixing problems and teach everyone to study problems methodically
- Master the practices being used so as to enable Kaizen and employee empowerment
- Use simple visual management to reveal problems and coordinate activities
- Use only well-tested technology that serves the people and the processes they use
- Grow leaders from within who thoroughly understand the work, live the philosophy and teach it to others
- Develop exceptional people and teams that understand and follow the company's philosophy
- Respect your extended network of partners by challenging them to grow and helping them to improve
- Go and see for yourself at the real place of work in order to understand the situation and provide useful help
- Make decisions slowly, by consensus, thoroughly considering all the options, then implement them rapidly
- Become and sustain a learning organization through relentless reflection and the practice of Kaizen

**Hot tip**

Kaizen is the Japanese practice that focuses on continuous improvement. The practice is covered on page 108.

# Lean Principles

The term 'Lean Software Development' originated in a book of the same name by Mary and Tom Poppendieck. The book presents the traditional lean principles in a modified form adapted to agile development practices. These were defined as the seven principles of lean software development and it will be seen that these follow on from the concepts set out in the previous topic:

## Eliminate Waste

By using the seven muda to examine the software development process, areas of waste should be identified. These can include unnecessary code, unwanted functionality, delays, poorly specified requirements and many more. Once identified the waste can then be eliminated.

## Amplify Learning

By continually feeding back information on what is happening at the work place to colleagues and customers, the results of the learning process can benefit the whole team.

## Decide as Late as Possible

By delaying decision making, uncertainty will be reduced and the decisions when made should therefore be better. This also means that some beneficial functionality can be built and delivered to the customer earlier.

## Deliver as Fast as Possible

Getting the product out to the customers as fast as possible means getting feedback from them as soon as possible. It also means they will start to benefit from the use of the product sooner.

## Empower the Team

Empower the team to make decisions about the work they do and the processes being used as close to the work place as possible.

## Build Integrity In

By building integrity into the software components they will work well together and not cause conflicts or issues. Refactoring also allows the code to be kept lean.

## See the Whole

By seeing the big picture the integration of the components and of work produced by different disparate groups can be achieved.

Each of these principles is expanded in the following seven topics.

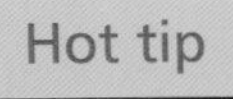


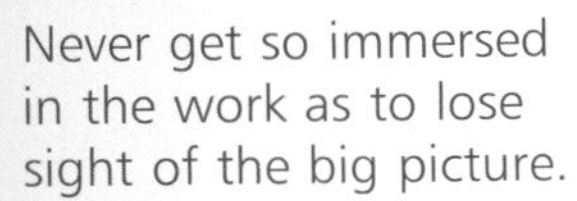
Never get so immersed in the work as to lose sight of the big picture.

# Eliminate Waste

Value has been defined as anything the customer is prepared to pay for. So anything not adding value to the customer is considered to be waste. In a software development environment this includes:

### Unnecessary Code

Unnecessary code or functionality is a waste. Partially done coding that is abandoned later in the development process is waste. Extra processes and features not used by customers are all waste.

### Delays

Any delay in the software development process is a waste. Waiting for other activities, teams or processes to be completed is a waste. Defects and lower quality cause delay and are waste. Filling out documentation or writing reports causes delay and are waste.

### Unclear Requirements

Poorly defined or imprecise requirements are a waste. They will either result in the wrong functions being developed or time being wasted while they are cleared up.

### Inadequate Testing

Insufficient or inadequate testing can lead to wasted work needing to be corrected or rewritten. Automated testing can help to eliminate this.

### Bureaucracy

Management bureaucracy, such as unnecessary documentation, that can hinder the rapid development of code is a waste.

### Poor Communication

Slow internal communication which can result in wasted effort or delays to work is a waste.

In order to be able to eliminate waste, we have to be able to recognize it. There are many techniques that can be used to examine a process and identify where value is added to the product. The same techniques can also be used to identify and recognize waste. If an activity could be skipped or the required results could still be achieved without it, then it is waste.

Having identified waste, the next step is to examine the sources and then eliminate them. This should be an iterative process until all non-essential processes and procedures have been removed.

**Hot tip**

Never stop looking for waste and then eliminating it.

# Amplify Learning

Software development is, by its very nature, a continuous learning process. It requires an exploratory approach for problem solving and the results of this will provide learning. When software is developed in a team environment this adds the challenge of spreading the learning throughout the team. The best approach for improving a software development team environment is by looking for ways to amplify or communicate the learning.

## Show and Tell

User requirements gathering is a process that can be simplified by developing basic screens, demonstrating them to the users and getting their feedback. In a similar way, different ideas can be tried by writing the code and showing the results to the users. This can be far more effective than adding more detailed design documentation or specifications. By running tests with the users as soon as the code is written the developers can get instant feedback and prevent any further wasted effort.

## Short Iterations

The learning process can also be accelerated by the use of short iteration cycles, each culminating in integration testing and customer demonstration. Improved customer feedback will help establish where the current phase of development is and what changes need to be made for future improvements. During these sessions the customer representatives and development team will learn more about any problems and review possible solutions for further development. This way the customer understands their needs better and the developers understand better how to satisfy those needs.

## Set-based Development

Another technique in the communication and learning process with the customer is the use of set-based development. This focuses on the constraints of the future solution and not the possible solutions. This promotes the development of the solution through dialog with the customer.

## Kaizen

Kaizen is Japanese for improvement. It is a practice that focuses on the continuous improvement of processes. It is based on a cycle of identifying problems (or opportunities), discussing them with colleagues, proposing improvements to the process and then implementing them. It is another way of amplifying learning.

# Decide Late

Software development is always associated with some degree of uncertainty. Therefore better results should be achieved by making decisions as late as possible in the process. This means all available options are kept open until the decision can be made based on facts and not on assumptions or predictions of outcomes.

The more complex the system, the more capacity for change should be built into it. This will enable the delay of important and crucial commitments until as late as possible.

Hot tip

Keep all your options open until you have to make a decision.

## Iterative Approach

The iterative and adaptive approach promotes this principle with the ability to adapt to changes as they become known and correct mistakes as they are identified. These changes and mistakes could otherwise be very costly to correct if they only come to light after the system is operational.

Due to its flexible nature, the lean software development approach can actually allow some functions to be built earlier for customers. This in turn can allow the delay of any crucial decisions until customers have fully understood their needs and potential solutions to them.

## Planning

In the lean development environment, planning activities should concentrate on the different options available based on the current situation. Once the different options have been costed in terms of time and other resources required for their implementation, the customer is likely to make a much better decision on the way forward. This once again provides the flexibility required for late decision making.

## Set-based Design

Another idea from Toyota is set-based design. If a new function is needed for any product, several teams will be asked to design solutions to the same requirement. Each team then learns about the requirement and designs a potential solution.

If any of the potential solutions are deemed unsuitable by the customer they are dropped. At the end of the designated period, the remaining designs are compared and the best is chosen, possibly with some modifications based on learning from the other teams.

Don't forget

Models and prototypes can help communicate potential solutions.

# Deliver Fast

Sometimes developing software seems to take forever. People hit problems and take a long time thinking about and fixing them. Or they make things complicated rather than keeping them simple.

In an era of rapid technological evolution, it is not the biggest that survives, but the fastest. The quicker the end product can be delivered, the sooner the customer can start to benefit from it and the sooner feedback can be received, for incorporation into the next iteration.

## Short Iterations

The shorter the iterations, the better the feedback, learning and communication within the team. With a shorter duration decisions can be delayed. Speed assures the fulfillment of the customer's present needs and not what they required yesterday or tomorrow. This gives them the opportunity to delay making up their minds about what they really require until they gain better knowledge of the potential final product. Customers also value rapid delivery of a quality product.

## Just In Time

The just in time production approach can be applied equally well to software development. The customer can present the required results to the team in a simple way using small requirements cards or user stories and then leave the team to organize itself and allocate the work.

The development team can then get on with estimating the time it will need for the implementation of each user story. The work organization becomes a self-pulling system. During the daily stand-up meeting, each member of the team reviews what they did yesterday, what that are going to do today and requests any input or support needed from colleagues or the customer.

## Set-based Design

Toyota's set-based design was introduced in the previous topic. This also enables fast delivery by the developers of parallel potential solutions rather than by trying one solution at a time with the inherent delay if the first potential solution is not suitable.

To deliver fast get the right people, keep the product simple, work as a team, eliminate waste and build in quality.

# Team Empowerment

The traditional belief about decision making in most businesses has always been that the managers tell the workers what to do and how to do their jobs. In fact in many businesses the managers are even referred to as the key decision makers.

## Work Out

In a work out technique, the roles are reversed. The managers are taught how to listen to the developers, so they can explain better what actions might be taken, as well as provide suggestions for improvements. The lean approach favors finding good people and letting them do their own jobs. The manager's role is to encourage progress, catch errors and remove any impediments. To facilitate the team but not to micro manage them.

## Human Resources

Another mistaken belief has been to consider people as resources. Even putting the word human in front of resources does not improve it. People might be resources from a statistical point of view, but in software development or any other 'knowledge worker' environment, people need something more than just a list of tasks they are to perform. They need motivation, peer esteem and some form of higher but achievable purpose to work for.

## Self-organization

In any agile environment, but most especially in a lean development environment, the development team should be able to organize themselves for how they can best work to achieve the required solution. Not just who does which task but the processes and procedures they use as well.

The allocation or selection of tasks should be based on the team members' skills and abilities. They should also help them to understand the whole project and develop their skills.

The team should also be able to elect a team leader to coordinate things and provide support and help in difficult situations, as well as making sure that morale and team spirit is maintained.

## Customer Access

The developers also need be given direct access to the customer to clarify requirements, demonstrate potential solutions and test the potential product. This is ideally achieved by imbedding the customer representatives in the team.

Full customer involvement and co-location are critical to success.

# Inbuilt Integrity

In addition to the product having functional integrity, it also needs to have a perceived integrity, conceptual integrity, architectural integrity and automated integrity testing:

## Perceived Integrity

The customer needs to have an overall understanding of the product that is being developed and how it will be used. This is called perceived integrity: how it will be advertised, delivered, deployed, accessed, how intuitive its use is, the price it will be sold for or how well it solves their problems.

## Conceptual Integrity

The conceptual integrity refers to how well the system's separate components will function together as a whole. This is best achieved by understanding each part of the problem and solving it at the same time, instead of sequentially. The means that the requirements are received by the developers in small batches and not all at once. It is best done via face-to-face communication and the information flow should be continuous in both directions, from the customer to development team and back. This is a far more effective way of developing software then handing over a large specification, waiting a considerable time while the developers are locked away coding it, and then receiving all the results back for testing at once.

## Architectural Integrity

One of the best ways of achieving architectural integrity is through refactoring. The more additional features are added to a product, the worse the code becomes for further improvements. Refactoring aims to keep code simple, clear and with the minimum number of features.

## Integrity Testing

In addition to an automated building process, development should be accompanied by a complete and automated test suite. At the end of the development process the product integrity should be verified with thorough testing. This will ensure that the product does what the customer expects it to.

As automated tests are part of the production process, if they do not add value to the product then they should be considered waste. So automated testing is a means to an end, specifically the reduction of defects, rather than a goal.

No part of the process is sacred, everything should be inspected for waste.

# See the Whole

Software products are not just the sum of their functions, but also the product of their interactions, i.e. how the different bits work when they are put together. Software defects also tend to accumulate during the development process. By breaking down the requirements or user stories into smaller tasks and by standardizing the different stages of development, the root causes of defects should be found and eliminated. But it is still important to keep sight of the whole or big picture.

## The Big Picture

The larger the system and the more disparate organizations that are involved in its development the greater the importance of having well defined relationships between the different suppliers. Even if the parts are developed by different teams in the same organization these criteria still apply.

At the end of the day the aim is to produce a system with smoothly interacting components. During a longer period of development it is much more critical to have a strong sub-contractor network than to optimize short-term profitability. The aim is to get everyone on the project, no matter who they work for, into a win-win relationship.

## Lean Thinking

Lean thinking has to be well understood by all the members of a project team before they begin to implement the required situation. This may indicate the need for some sort of workshop on the principles if they are not all from the same background.

"Think big, act small, fail fast and learn rapidly"

This the slogan that sums up lean principles throughout the whole software development process. Seeing the big picture is the starting point in this. Small increments and tasks satisfy the second part. Delivering fast ensures that failures are spotted quickly so they can be rectified. Amplified learning ensures that everyone in the team learns quickly and effectively from each other's learnings.

Only when all the lean principles are implemented together, combined with a good common sense approach and with respect for the working environment, is there a basis for success in software development.

# Summary

- Lean software development has evolved from the lean production processes developed in the automotive industry
- The basis of lean philosophy is the elimination of waste, where waste is defined as anything that does not create value for the customer
- Lean software development has inherited the approach and philosophy and gone on to define seven principles: eliminate waste, amplify learning, decide as late as possible, deliver as fast as possible, empower the team, build integrity in and see the whole
- Eliminating waste from the development process is by removing: unnecessary code, delays, unclear requirements, inadequate testing, bureaucracy and poor communication
- Software development is a continuous learning process and this learning should be amplified by sharing it as often as possible with the customer and the team
- Making decisions as late as possible removes uncertainty, allows options to be kept open and ensures that decisions are made based on fact and a more complete understanding of the problems
- Delivering as quickly as possible means that the customer can start to get benefit from the product sooner and provide feedback more quickly
- Empowering the team turns the traditional management approach on its head and makes the best use of the people in the team
- Building integrity into the product and the processes used is achieved by the customer having a perceived integrity, by face-to-face communications achieving conceptual integrity, refactoring keeping the product simple and automated testing keeping the product bug free
- It is important to see the whole (the big picture) and to keep all parts of the development team working towards the same aim, particularly if it is a dispersed or multi-supplier team

# 7 Getting Started

*You have only one opportunity to start up a project so it is worth getting it right first time. This chapter lists the first key steps in establishing the feasibility of a project.*

# Methods & Deliverables

Hot tip

XP and Lean are specifically software development methods, whereas DSDM and Scrum are applicable to any development project.

In the previous four chapters we examined four of the more popular development methodologies: DSDM, Scrum, XP and Lean Development. While there is a significant overlap and compatibility between these methodologies, they all have their own focus and their own terminology. They also tend to refer to different deliverables and sometimes the same deliverable but with a different name.

From a project management perspective DSDM is the most complete of these methodologies so this chapter and the next three chapters will use the DSDM life cycle and product names to describe the deliverables to be produced. If your project is using other methodologies the names and contents may be slightly different but in essence the deliverables will still be the same.

None of the deliverables should be considered mandatory and if it does not add value to the project it should not be used. The following deliverables will be covered:

## Pre-Project

Before the project starts there is one recommended deliverable:

- Terms of Reference (for the project)

## Feasibility

The first (optional) phase produces two deliverables:

- Feasibility Assessment (the requirements and business case)
- Outline Plan (how it will be carried out)

## Foundations

This phase establishes the foundations for the project and may include any or all of the following deliverables:

- Business Foundations (expands on the feasibility assessment)
- Prioritized Requirements List (expands on the requirements)
- Solution Foundations (the type of solution required)
- Management Foundations (how the project will be run)
- Delivery Plan (developed from the outline plan)
- Delivery Control Pack (how the project will be controlled)

## Exploration & Engineering

Development is where the majority of the project work is done and the solution is developed. It produces six new deliverables:

- Timebox Plan (for each timebox)
- Solution Assurance Pack (test plan)
- Evolving Solution (the developed product)
- Deployment Plan (how the product will be implemented)
- Benefits Realization Plan (how the benefits can be measured)
- Timebox Review Record (how the timebox worked out)

It also updates three earlier deliverables to reflect changes to the business requirements and developed solution:

- Prioritized Requirements List
- Delivery Control Pack
- Delivery Plan

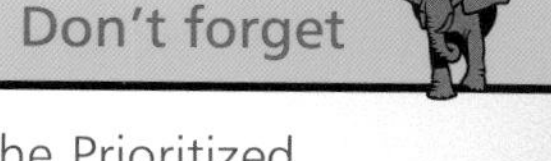


The Prioritized Requirements List is referred to as the Product Backlog in Scrum.

## Deployment

The deployment phase implements the developed product and produces two new deliverables:

- Deployed Solution (increments and the final product)
- Project Review Report (after the final deployment)

It also updates four earlier deliverables to reflect changes to what is being deployed and how:

- Delivery Control Pack
- Deployment Plan
- Solution Assurance Pack
- Delivery Control Pack

## Post Project

After the final product is deployed there is one final deliverable:

- Benefits Assessment (did the solution meet the business case)

# Pre-Project

Projects can come into being for a number of different reasons: a new business requirement; a problem that requires a project to address it; a better way of doing something and many other reasons. But regardless of how or why a project has come into being it needs to be set up correctly if it is going to be successful.

The pre-project phase is intended to formalize the project proposal so that it can be considered by the business in the context of other things that could be done with the money and resources the project will require.

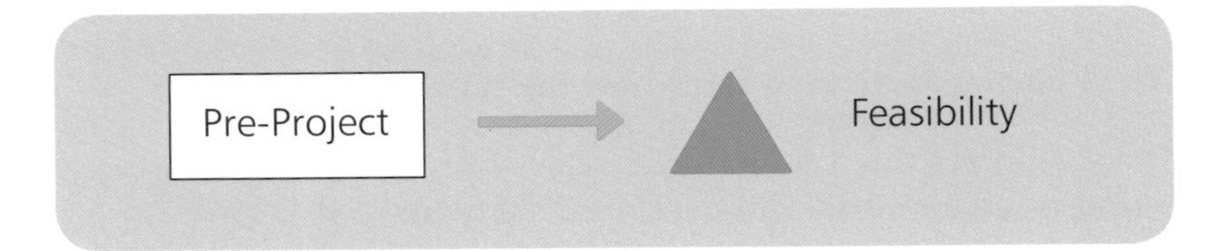


## Objectives

The first things that need to be defined are the objectives of the project, what it is intended to achieve. The objectives of the project should describe:

1. The business problem or requirement that the project is intended to address
2. The identities of the business project sponsor and the business visionary
3. How the project fits in with and helps to support the business strategy
4. The scope, plan and required resources for the feasibility phase of the project

The pre-project phase should be fairly short. Its prime purpose is to create the terms of reference. This should be a short document (one or two pages at the most) that justifies carrying out the feasibility phase of the project. It should not attempt to justify the whole project as that is what will be done in the feasibility phase of the project.

## Terms of Reference

The terms of reference is a short document that sets out the objectives of the project together with the business reasons for carrying it out. The sole purpose of the document is to justify the initial feasibility phase which will determine whether or not the project is feasible. It should contain the answers to five questions:

1. What are the objectives of the project and what are the business reasons (drivers) for carrying it out?
2. What is the outline scope of the project?
3. What dependencies and constraints have been identified?
4. What resources will be required to carry out the feasibility phase and establish if the project is feasible?
5. What funding will be required and what is the justification for it?

## Quality Criteria

The quality criteria for the document are as follows:

- Has the business justification for the project been established?
- Do the objectives support the business justification?
- Is the scope for the feasibility phase clear?
- Have any constraints been explained?
- Are the work effort and timescale for the feasibility phase realistic?
- Have all other requirements for the phase been identified?
- Have the people who will work on or be impacted by the feasibility phase been identified?

The terms of reference can be produced by anyone suitable in the business but it needs to be accepted by the project manager and business analyst and approved by the business project sponsor. There is an example terms of reference on the next page.

Hot tip

Make sure all the quality criteria are satisfied before submitting the terms of reference for approval.

# Terms of Reference

The following is an example of a terms of reference document for West Country Tours, a holiday company. The business has been running for a couple of years and has a company web site but they are starting to suffer as they cannot take on-line bookings.

Hot tip

A template for terms of reference is provided for your use on our website. Go to www.ineasysteps.com/resource-centre/downloads

## Terms of Reference

This document sets out the objectives for a proposed on-line booking system for West Country Tours.

### Objectives

The business is starting to lose sales due to the absence of an on-line booking system. The business aim is to be the top tour operator in the South West and this cannot be achieved unless on-line bookings can be processed in real time.

This project is therefore being sponsored by Bill Bounce and the business visionary is Susan Stills. As the first step a short study is proposed in order to establish the feasibility of the project.

### Project Scope

The project will investigate and make proposals for the speedy introduction of the new functionality to cover on-line booking, payment and confirmation.

### Dependencies and Constraints

The project will require external resources to develop the required software and must be operational in time for the start of the peak booking season (New Year).

### Resource Requirements

This will require one full-time person for 20 days to conduct the study, together with time from the business visionary and other business staff equivalent to another 20 days.

### Funding Required

No external funding is required for the feasibility study but the nominal cost of staff time should be recognized so a budget of $18,000 is requested.

Hot tip

Always recognize the cost of internal people working on a project as they are a business cost.

# Feasibility Phase

The purpose of the feasibility phase is to establish whether or not the proposed project is viable from both a technical and business perspective. In order to achieve this the requirements (as defined in the terms of reference) must be investigated together with the potential solutions to those requirements complete with timescales and costs.

## Deliverables

There are two main deliverables from the feasibility phase: the feasibility assessment and the outline project plan. In addition, if the business case has not already been documented in the pre-project phase, it will also need to be produced.

## Objectives

The following are the main objectives for the phase and the steps that will need to be completed to achieve them:

1. To establish whether or not there is a feasible solution to the business requirements as set out in the terms of reference document
2. To identify the benefits that are likely to flow from delivery of the project
3. To establish the possible alternatives for delivery of the solution together with the resources that will be required to deliver them, including project management
4. To define the required project organization and its governance
5. To produce outline estimates of the likely timescale and costs of the project
6. To produce a plan and resources for the next (foundation) phase of the project

The feasibility phase should be kept as short as possible. Its sole purpose is to establish whether or not it is worth proceeding to the foundations phase.

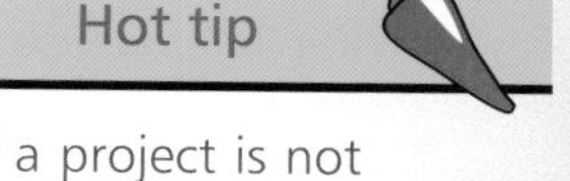


If a project is not feasible then it should be stopped immediately.

# Feasibility Assessment

The feasibility assessment documents the results of the feasibility study. It should include a high-level overview of the project together with an assessment of its feasibility from a technical and business viewpoint. It should also include details of any significant risks that have been identified together with the planned risk mitigation strategy for dealing with them.

The feasibility assessment should cover the following:

1. Outline descriptions of one or more solutions most likely to meet the business requirements and objectives
2. Any other potential solutions that have been or could be considered with an indication of the reason for not recommending them
3. Description of the major products or deliverables to be produced by the project
4. Documentation of any technical standards, regulatory or legal compliance the proposed solution could be subject to
5. The expected life and maintainability requirements for the proposed solution
6. The business vision for the successful outcome of the project
7. The expected cost budget for the project together with the quantified benefits expected to flow from it
8. Critical success factors for the delivery timescale, cost and scope and any desirable but not essential functionality
9. Details of all assumptions that have been made and constraints that have been identified
10. Details of all identified risks that could have an impact on the project or business

The feasibility assessment consists of three main deliverables: the outline business case, outline solution and an optional feasibility prototype.

### Outline Business Case

The outline business case is a high-level document that sets out the justification for the project. It should contain the business vision for success, the scope and objectives of the proposed project, any assumptions, dependencies and risks, any discarded alternatives, the major deliverables and the estimated costs and benefits of the project.

Hot tip

Examples of these three deliverables are illustrated over the following three topics.

### Outline Solution

The outline solution should be a high-level description of the proposed solution (or solutions) to meet the outline business case. It should also define any technical constraints to which the solution will have to adhere.

### Feasibility Prototype

A feasibility prototype is a 'throw-away' model of the proposed solution or some features of it. Its purpose is to illustrate how the proposed solution could eventually work.

### Quality Criteria

The following quality criteria should be considered for each of the proposed solutions:

- Are the business objectives which will be met by the proposed solution clearly defined?
- Will the solution allow the business benefits to be achieved?
- Is the proposed solution technically feasible?
- Can the project be delivered within the costs and timescale set out in the business case?
- Have all the key project stakeholders been identified and were they involved in the outline business case?
- Is the business case clear enough to enable the project sponsor to make a decision to proceed?
- Is the scope of the project defined well enough for refinement in the foundations phase?

# Business Case

The business case should contain the justification for carrying out the project as opposed to doing something else with the money or doing nothing. It should include the business vision of what the project will deliver, the objectives and scope of the project, any assumptions, dependencies and risks, the main deliverables and the estimated costs and benefits. The following is an example of a business case for West Country Tours:

**Business Case**
This document sets out the justification for the proposed on-line booking project based on the estimated cost and anticipated business benefits to be gained.

**Vision**
On completion of the project it is envisaged that potential customers who have identified a holiday from our brochure or web site will be able to check availability and make an on-line booking including payment of a deposit or the full balance.

**Objectives & Scope**
To implement an on-line availability checking, booking and payment system to interface with the existing web site and back office systems. The required functionality must be in place for the start of the New Year.

**Assumptions**
It is assumed that the project management and development work will be contracted out but all other project roles will be provided by our own staff.

**Dependencies & Risks**
That suitable resources can be obtained for the contracted out roles and staff can be freed from other duties where required. If these resources are not available the project will not be viable.

**Deliverables**
The main deliverable from the project will be a fully operational on-line booking and payment system together with interfaces to existing systems. There must be adequate documentation to allow for the on-going operation and support of the system.

**Cost & Benefits**
Based on current estimates the expected cost of the project will be $250,000 to$500,000. The anticipated business benefit will be at least $250,000 per year so the project will pay for itself within two to three years and produce net benefit thereafter.

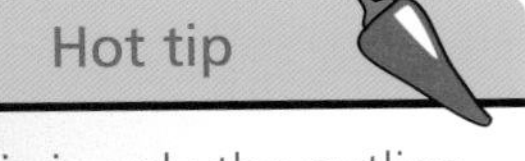


This is only the outline business case so estimates should be kept broad.

# Outline Solution

The outline solution gives a high-level description of the probable structure of the overall solution, what it includes and excludes and an overview of the proposed solution architecture. It will also specify any technical constraints which the proposed solution must comply with.

If more than one solution is being proposed then there will be an outline solution for each of the proposed solutions. The following is an example of an outline solution for West Country Tours:

**Outline Solution**
This document sets out the proposed solution to support the outline business case. It will be used with the business case to justify continuing with the project or stopping it.

**Project Approach**
Given the critical timescale of the project it is proposed that the project is run as an agile development. This will ensure that the solution will be delivered to the business on time with as many of the prioritized requirements as can be included in the time and budget available.

**Main Deliverables**
Holiday availability: confirms or offers alternatives if not available.

On-line booking: the customer confirms the holiday booking.

Payment: customer is asked to pay a deposit or full payment.

Confirmation: customer is sent the necessary documentation.

Integration: to existing systems.

**Delivery**
The required functionality will be delivered through iterative and incremental product releases. Each release will implement the next set of agreed top priority functions.

**Product Life**
The proposed product should have an expected life of five to ten years so must be a quality product with good maintainability.

**Risk Analysis**
The proposed project approach requires a high level of business involvement in the development. One member of the business team will need to be located with the developers full-time for the duration of the project. If this commitment cannot be made the project will not be achievable in the required time frame.



Hot tip

Always make sure you get full business involvement committed for the duration of the project.

# Feasibility Prototype

The feasibility prototype is a 'throw away' model or prototype of the proposed solution or parts of it. It is intended to aid the understanding of the proposed solution. It can demonstrate the technical approach to complex parts of the requirements or provide an illustration of how the proposed solution might work. In the case of the example illustrated in the previous two topics, it might consist of working, partially working or even dummy applications to illustrate how the requirements could be met. The following screens were produced in XHTML to illustrate how the application could look and feel.

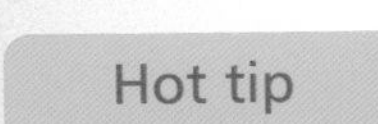

Hot tip

Prototypes can be produced using any available tool or even hand drawn.

## Holiday Availability

The first prototype is a screen to confirm the holiday requirements entered by the customer and offer them available dates for the holiday they have specified:

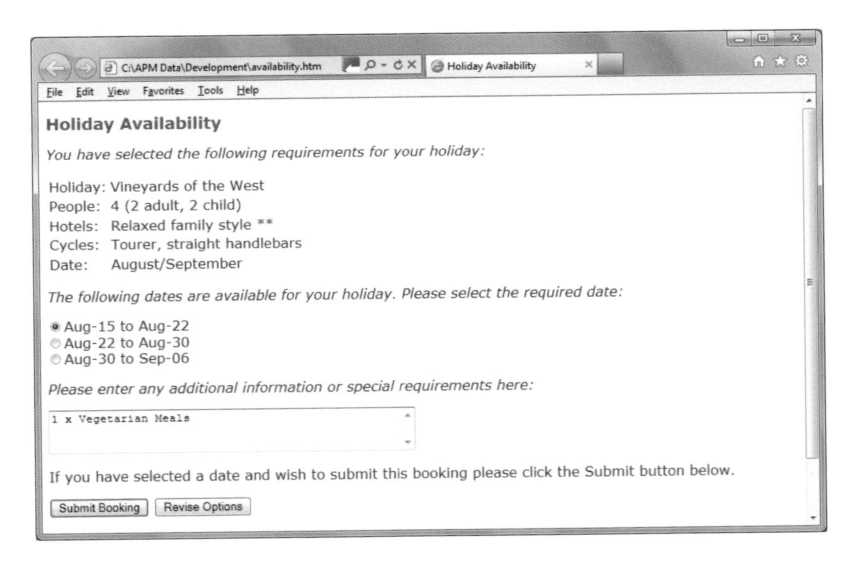


The following tests will be applied to this function:

- Customer selects required date and submits booking
- Customer selects date, adds additional information and submits booking
- Customer selects Revise Options
- Customer selects date, adds additional information and selects Revise Options

## Make Payment

After the customer submits their booking from the holiday availability screen they will be taken to the payment screen:

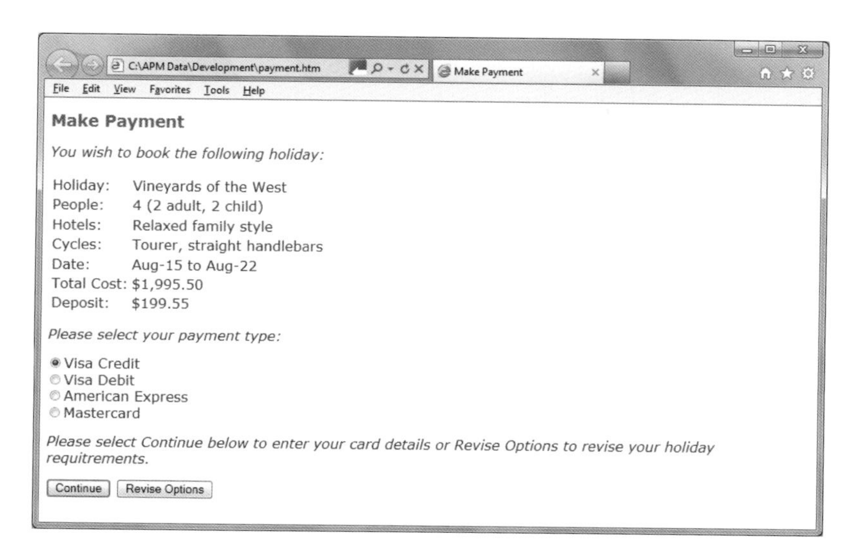


The following tests will be applied to this function:

- Customer selects required payment type and continues
- Customer clicks continue without selecting a payment type
- Customer clicks revise options
- Customer selects payment type and clicks revise options

For each of the valid options on these two screens the customer should be taken directly to the next appropriate screen.

For any invalid options (e.g. customer selects continue without selecting a payment type) a warning should be displayed on the same screen in red, with instructions as to the correct action required (i.e. please select a payment type before clicking continue).

For any ambiguous options (e.g. customer selects date, adds additional information and then selects revise options) a suitable warning should be displayed on the same screen. "Do you want to cancel the information you have already entered and go back to start the selection process again?" With a Yes/No option.

This is just an example of a feasibility prototype, it is not expected to be complete.

# Outline Plan

The outline plan is produced to provide a high-level overview of the whole project together with a more detailed plan for the next (foundations) phase.

## Plan Content

The following is the suggested list of contents for the outline plan. They may not all be required and there may be other items that should be included:

1. An overview of the approach to be taken by the project and the methodologies to be used
2. Preliminary work estimates together with a list of the people or skills that will be required to complete the work and the preliminary cost estimates
3. A list of the key project deliverables together with their acceptance criteria
4. Facilities, tools and support systems that will be required to support the development process
5. The organization of the project team and the project governance to be applied
6. Details of any risks to the project or to the implementation of the developed solution
7. An outline schedule for the overall project, showing the main project milestones for the delivery and deployment of the solution

The plan should give management a good overview of the whole proposed project with the processes and methods being used. It should give a clear indication of the expected timescale, resource requirements and costs. It should state the proposed deliverables with their quality and acceptance criteria. Finally it should outline the potential risks to the project. This should allow the business to consider the project and make any required decisions.

## Foundations Phase Plan

In addition to the outline plan, the detailed plan for the next (foundations) phase of the project also needs to be developed. This plan should include the following:

1. The objectives and scope for the phase
2. The project team, together with their roles and responsibilities
3. The deliverables from the phase and how the project team will go about producing them
4. The key tasks and activities that will be need to be carried out in the phase
5. The detailed schedule for the phase
6. A list of any assumptions, constraints and risks that could have an impact on the scope, delivery or quality of the work and delivered products

This document, together with the outline project plan, should enable the relevant stakeholders to agree to the project and the project sponsor to approve the start of the foundations phase. As part of the approval process the following quality criteria should be satisfied:

- Is the overall approach to project management and solution delivery appropriate and achievable?
- Are the estimates for time, resources and costs realistic?
- Do the project timelines meet the critical success factors as set out in the outline business case?
- Are the proposed control, risk management and product quality assurance processes suitable for the project?
- Is everything specified for the foundations phase in place and available to the project in the timelines specified?

**Don't forget**

Make sure that any plan satisfies the quality criteria before submitting it for approval.

# Summary

- Project phases and deliverables are defined using DSDM terminology as this has good project management coverage
- Before starting the project (pre-project phase) make sure the terms of reference for the project are defined
- The terms of reference should include the objectives, scope, business drivers, dependencies and constraints together with the resource and budget requirements for the first (feasibility) phase of the project
- The feasibility phase establishes whether or not the project is viable from both a technical and a business perspective. It results in the production of a feasibility assessment and an outline project plan
- The feasibility assessment sets out the potential solutions to the requirements together with the outline business case for carrying the project out. It consists of three parts: the outline business case, the outline solution and an optional 'throw-away' solution prototype
- The outline business case states the justification for the project together with the estimated cost of the project and the expected benefits of carrying it out
- The outline solution defines how the requirements will be met, the project approach, any technical or other constraints, the main deliverables and how they will be released
- Feasibility prototypes or models may be produced to help demonstrate how possible solutions might look or function or to aid the understanding of the technical approach
- The outline project plan is a high-level plan for the whole project setting out the approach, preliminary work estimates, deliverables, tools and facilities required and an outline schedule for when the major project milestones will occur
- The foundations phase plan is a detailed plan for the next phase of the project and will include the project team with their roles and responsibilities, phase deliverables, key tasks, the detailed schedule and any risks or assumptions that could have an impact on the phase

# 8 Foundations

*This chapter deals with the Foundations Phase and its deliverables. Its purpose is to establish a firm set of foundations for the project.*

# Objectives

The foundations phase sets out to establish the foundations of the project in terms of the business requirement, solution development and project management. At this early stage of the project it is critical that the investigations do not get into too much detail. In essence what it must do is to demonstrate that the needs of the business can be met without necessarily demonstrating how it will be done.

The objectives of the phase are defined as follows:

1. To create a baseline of the high-level requirements for the project and establish their priority in terms of their relevance to the business needs
2. To explain the business processes that the proposed solution will need to support
3. To identify the data or information that will be created, updated and used by the proposed solution
4. To describe that strategies that will be used for the deployment and implementation of the proposed solution
5. To develop further and expand on the business case for the project
6. To begin the design of the architecture that will be used by the proposed solution and identify its infrastructure and physical aspects
7. To define the technical implementation standards that the solution will need to follow
8. To explain how quality assurance will be carried out on the project and its deliverables
9. To set out the project and management organization structure for the project and the project governance that will be implemented to control it

10. To define the solution development life-cycle that will be used for the project

11. To describe the techniques that will be used for managing the project and measuring and communicating progress

12. To create a baseline of the schedule for the development and deployment of the solution

13. To identify and evaluate the risks to the project together with the plan for managing them

The foundations phase should be scheduled in a fixed timebox and every effort should be made to complete it on time. Where necessary the deliverables should only be developed as much as time permits. The aim is to allow the project to move on to the first part of the development (the exploration phase) as scheduled rather than trying to complete every deliverable perfectly.

## Business Input

The business will need to provide a significant amount of input during the foundations phase. The business representatives who will be involved in and provide input to the project need to be identified so that their level of commitment can be assured by the business management.

## Business Case

At the end of the foundations phase the business case, which sets out the justification for the project, needs to be reviewed, based on what is now known about the project. This should then result in one of two decisions:

- If the business case is still sound then the decision can be made to continue work on the project
- If the business case is not sound (e.g. too expensive, fewer benefits, too much risk) then the project should be stopped

If the project is to continue, then the project manager should confirm that everything is in place (or planned to be in place) ready for the start of the next (exploration) phase.

**Hot tip**

Stopping a project if it no longer has a clear justification is a good outcome for the foundations phase.

# Business Foundations

The business foundations document sets out all the important information about the business that is critical to the success of the project. It needs to be understood and agreed by all the project stakeholders before the proposed solution is developed. It consists of two parts: the business vision and the business case.

## Business Vision

This part of the document sets out how the business is expected to operate after the proposed solution has been developed. It should describe:

1. The future vision of the business as it will be after the project has been completed. This should be a high-level outline in a few paragraphs
2. The ways in which that view of the business is different from the current position
3. How the proposed project will contribute to this new business vision
4. Any other projects or activities (current or planned) that are a part of or could have an impact on that vision

It should not give any requirements for the proposed solution, just describe how the solution is expected to contribute to the vision.

## Business Case

The second part of the document is a refinement of the outline business case to provide the business justification for the project. It should provide the following:

1. The quantified benefits that the project is expected to deliver
2. The summarized costs of the project and the proposed project budget
3. A cost/benefit analysis based on the quantified benefits and summarized costs to justify the project

4. The critical success factors for the project in terms of: time, cost and scope

5. A list of the requirements which are within scope but desirable rather than essential (i.e. should have and could have requirements)

6. A description of how the proposed solution fits with the business strategies and standards and any assumptions that have been made

## Quality Criteria

The document should satisfy the following quality criteria:

- Is the business vision clearly stated and unambiguous?
- Have all the key project stakeholders reviewed and accepted the business vision?
- Are the beneficiaries of the project identified and have they been involved in the business case?
- Is it clear how the costs and benefits have been calculated?
- Have the benefits been identified and quantified in such a way that will allow them to be measured now to establish a benefits baseline?
- Is it clear how the benefits will be measured in future to assess the achievement of the benefits?
- Has the relationship between benefits and scope been defined so that the impact of reducing scope can be assessed?
- Has the business case been made clearly enough to enable the project sponsor to decide whether to continue?

## Production & Approval

The document should be produced by the business analyst with input from all the relevant business stakeholders. Costs and benefits should be accepted by the business stakeholders with final approval given by the project sponsor.

# Requirements List

The prioritized requirements list (PRL) defines the requirements that the project needs to deliver together with an assessment of their priority. They are specified at a fairly high level and are prioritized (using the MoSCoW rules) based on how important they are towards meeting the project objectives.

The PRL effectively defines the overall scope of the project and it should be baselined at the end of the foundations phase, but it will continue to be developed by refinement of detail during the exploration and engineering phases. It should also identify the minimum usable subset for the first deployment of the product.

## Quality Criteria

The prioritized requirements list should satisfy the following quality criteria:

- Do the requirements address all aspects of the proposed solution and so define the overall scope of the project?
- Have the requirements that represent the minimum usable subset of features for the first deployment of the product been identified?
- Have the solution development team members and the business representatives collaborated to agree the priorities?
- Have the MoSCoW rules been applied correctly to allow the solution development team to guarantee the delivery of all the must have and the majority of the should have requirements?

Hot tip

A template for a prioritized requirements list for your use is provided on our website. Go to www.ineasysteps.com/resource-centre/downloads

## Development

The requirements list should be developed by the business analyst in collaboration with the business representatives. It should be accepted by the contributors, the solution development team and the project manager. Finally it should be approved on behalf of the business by the business visionary.

## Usage

Although initially created and baselined in the foundations phase the prioritized requirements list will be used and updated throughout the exploration, engineering and deployment phases.

An example of a partial requirements list for the West Country Tours project is illustrated opposite.

### Requirements List

Browse Holidays: 'Check Availability' function is available on all holiday browsing screens (Must Have).

Check Holiday Availability: client clicks 'check availability' and enters details of party, type of accommodation and target dates. System displays availability (Must Have).

Request More Information: if at any stage client feels unable to make booking system prompts them to request more information for follow up (Should Have).

Book Holiday: client selects required date from the available list, clicks Book Holiday and is taken to payment function (Must Have).

Pay Deposit/Balance: client books holiday and is taken to payment screen. Selects payment type and amount and confirms payment details and payment (Must Have).

Get Client ID: system uses client details to check client database and get ID if match found. If no match asks client if they are new (Must Have).

Create New Client: client prompted to enter their full details, system creates a new client on the client database and gives the client their ID (Must Have).

Thank Client: system thanks client and displays confirmed booking screen for client to print (Must Have).

Get Client Feedback: following booking the system prompts client to take part in a short survey on the booking process (Should Have).

Process Booking: system passes booking details to main booking system and confirms receipt (Must Have).

Track Booking Progress: 'Track Progress' function is available on all main screens. Client clicks and enters Client ID. System gets current status and displays with option for client to request contact (Could Have).



Hot tip

These are high level requirements and will, when refined, lead to additional Should and Could Haves.

# Solution Foundations

The solution foundations are intended to set out the basis of the solution that is to be developed. It needs to be understood and agreed by the development team and business representatives before the development work starts.

Don't produce anything unless it adds value to the project.

It is broken down into four areas, each of which should only be created if it adds value to the project:

- Business Area Definition
- System Architecture Definition
- Development Approach Definition
- Solution Prototype

## Business Area Definition

The business area definition needs to be produced for any project where the proposed solution will have an impact on the existing business processes. It is intended to provide the business context for the project and describes the business processes as they are currently and as they will be following the project.

The business area definition should be produced by the business analyst and will typically contain descriptions of the following:

- Business information or data that will be used, created or changed by the proposed solution
- Impact that the proposed solution will have on the business processes, organization, culture and resourcing
- Strategy to be used for deploying the increments of the solution in the business
- Training strategy for the people impacted by the proposed solution (the business end users)
- Business processes that will need to be changed
- New business processes that will be introduced

## System Architecture Definition

The system architecture definition is required for any information technology aspects of the project. It should define the technical framework the system will be developed in and the structure of the proposed solution. It should be produced by the technical co-ordinator and will typically contain descriptions of the following:

- Technical architecture to be used for the development and deployment of the proposed solution
- Development and target environment
- Computer hardware, infrastructure and network
- Software objects and components and their interactions
- Security and control aspects such as access policy

## Development Approach

The development approach definition sets out the standards that will be applied to the development of the solution and its testing. The development standards should be defined by the technical co-ordinator and the test standards by a member of the test team. They will typically contain descriptions of the following:

- Development standards, styles and practices to be applied during development of the solution
- Configuration management for the technical deliverables
- Technical test strategy for unit testing and integration testing
- Business test strategy for user acceptance testing

## Solution Prototype

The solution prototype is an optional element of the solution foundations which may demonstrate how the solution will work or certain aspects of it. It will be produced by the solution development team and will typically provide:

- A first-cut view of the solution or selected parts of it
- Demonstration of the effectiveness of the technical implementation standards
- View of how the solution may impact on current business processes and procedures
- Basis for agreement with the project stakeholders about the planned direction the project is taking

Hot tip

Prototypes will always aid communication and understanding with the business.

# Management Foundations

The management foundations document describes project governance and how the project will be organized and managed. It should also describe the agile methods and techniques that will be applied. It is a refinement of the outline plan produced in the feasibility phase.

## Objectives

The project objectives and success criteria (as set out in the outline plan) should be validated with the business and solution development team. They should then be developed and refined further based on any feedback received.

## Project Approach

This should set out the basic approach to the project, covering whether the solution is to be purchased or developed. If the solution is purchased it should state whether it will require customizing or configuration and if so whether this work will be carried out in-house or contracted out. If the solution is to be developed it should again state whether this will be in-house or contracted out. In all cases where external contractors are being used it should also set out how the contract will be managed.

It should describe where and how contingency is to be built into the project by reference to the three key constraints: time, cost and scope. Where the project involves changes to the business it should set out how these changes will be managed. Finally it should describe the project approach to prioritization of requirements, timeboxing of product delivery, iterative development and any other techniques such as facilitated workshops.

## Project Organization

This section should identify the key individuals in the project with their roles and responsibilities:

- Project Sponsor
- Business Visionary
- Project Manager
- Technical Co-ordinator
- Team Leader(s)

- Business Ambassador(s)
- Business Analyst
- Solution Developers
- Solution Testers

## Project Management

This section should set out how the work of the project is to be managed together with any supporting processes. In particular it should define how the following project management practices will be implemented:

- Risk Management
- Configuration Management
- Change Control
- Monitoring and Control
- Communication and Reporting
- Issue Management and Escalation Procedure

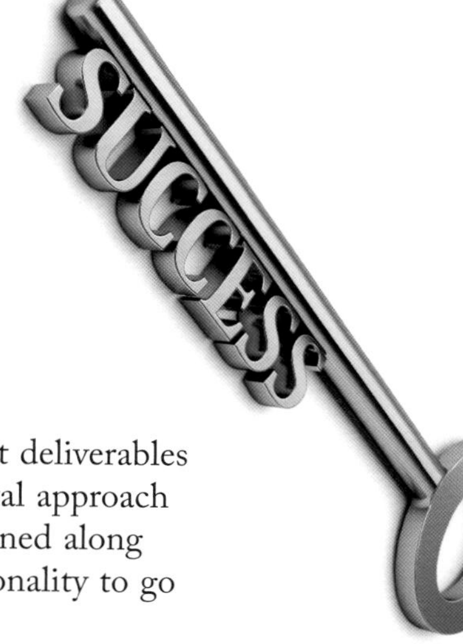


## Key Deliverables

This should contain an overview of all the key product deliverables and the main project milestones. Where an incremental approach to product delivery is being used this should be explained along with the technique to be used for selecting the functionality to go into each product release.

## Project Dependencies

The final section should list any major project dependencies with the way they will be managed.

## Quality Criteria

In summary the management foundations document should clarify how the solution is to be sourced, the management structure of the project including management of external resources, the people who will be working on the project (with their roles and responsibilities), the project governance mechanisms and the project management practices. It should be produced by the project manager, accepted by the senior members of the project team and approved by the project sponsor.

# Delivery Plan

The delivery plan is developed from the schedule in the outline plan and adds more detail to the schedule. It should cover all aspects of the development and deployment of the solution and consist of the schedule for each timebox together with any other non-timebox related activities. It should describe:

- The incremental approach to the project and the dates of each increment
- Dates of each deployment of the solution and any other milestone dates
- The schedule and focus for each of the development timeboxes
- Timing and dependencies for all activities which take place outside of the development timeboxes
- Resources allocated to the timebox and non-timebox activities
- Contingency that has been built into the three constraint areas (scope, time and cost)

## Quality Criteria

The delivery plan should be produced by the project manager in consultation with the development team and business representatives. It should satisfy the following quality criteria:

- Does the delivery plan list what will be delivered when and who is responsible for its delivery?
- Have all the required resources been identified?
- Is there a realistic approach to contingency bearing in mind the level of risk associated with the project?
- Can the delivery plan be used to track progress and communicate on it?

## Creation & Approval

The delivery plan should be produced by the project manager. It is critical that it is reviewed and accepted by all members of the project team and any other stakeholders. Once that has been completed it should then be approved by the business visionary on behalf of the business.

# Delivery Control

The delivery control package refers to the collection of logs, reports and documents that will be used to record and control the progress and status of the project. It should include at least the first three, if not all, of the following:

### Risk Log

The project risk log will record all of the risks identified before and during the project. It will also record the severity of each risk, what countermeasures are being taken and by whom.

Hot tip

Risk Log and Change Control are covered in the next two topics.

### Change Control

The change control record should identify and track all requests for changes to the scope of the project, together with the decision made and the outcome. Changes to the detail or understanding of a requirement will not be recorded only changes in the scope.

### Progress Reports

These are the periodic reports that track the progress of the project against the plan, track resource usage and cost against budget and highlight any current risks or issues.

### Issue Log

Issues are the things that go wrong on a project, things that were not included in the plan although they may hopefully be in the risk log. For this reason they are sometimes referred to as 'matured risks'. Like the risk log the issue log should track them and the countermeasures taken to resolve them.

### Communications Log

The communications log is a record of all formal communications (reports) or presentations. If a communication plan has been produced for the project the communications log will track its delivery.

### Burndown Charts

Burndown charts are a graphical record of progress that show the amount of work still remaining at a given point in time.

### Project Dashboard

Named after a car dashboard, a project dashboard will usually have a number of visual indicators of a project's status. These could be in the form of a dial, a bar chart, a pie chart and of course a burndown chart.

# Risk Log

A risk is defined as anything that could have a negative impact on the project. The risk log is a continuously updated record of all identified risks, with what has or is being done about each of them and their current status. An initial risk assessment should have been carried out as part of the feasibility phase to identify any 'show-stoppers'. The risk log itself should be created in the foundations phase.

## Risk Analysis

Risk analysis refers to the process of identifying risks, estimating their potential impact on the project and evaluating what can be done about them. It consists of three steps:

1. Risk identification is the process of identifying all risks to the project and business, it should be on-going for the life of the project
2. Risk estimation is the process of determining how critical a risk is, normally by estimating its probability and impact on a low, medium or high scale
3. Risk evaluation is the process of deciding what, if any, countermeasures to take to mitigate the risk

## The Risk Log

All of the above steps should be recorded in the risk log, together with information such as:

- A description of the risk
- The person who identified it
- The date is was first identified and the date of any subsequent updates to it
- The probability of it occurring (low, medium or high) and the impact it will have if it does occur (low, medium or high)
- The countermeasures being taken and the person responsible for them
- The current status of the risk

Review the risk log regularly.

# Change Control

The change control process is designed to record and track all requested changes to the project scope. It is not intended to track changes to the detail or understanding of requirements as these will happen through the life of the project as models, prototypes and the products are developed. Change control should be exercised through the following steps:

1. Confirm that the change is in reality a change to the scope of the project which will require a change to the high-level prioritized requirements list baselined in the foundations phase
2. Estimate the work effort that will be required to implement the change request and assess it for the impact it will have on the project's cost, time and scope tolerances
3. Assess the change request for the impact it will have on the technical architecture of the proposed solution, its security and performance
4. Assess the change request for the impact it will have on the business benefits as stated in the business case
5. If the change can be made within the agreed project tolerances the project manager can decide whether or not to make the change
6. If that change would take the project outside of the agreed tolerances it will need to be escalated to the project sponsor to make the decision
7. If the change request is approved then it should be prioritized and added to the prioritized requirements list for consideration in the next iteration

The change requests should be produced by the business analyst in consultation with the business representatives. They will then be approved, rejected or deferred by the project manager or sponsor.

**Don't forget**

Change should be welcomed in an agile project but the business needs to understand its potential impact.

# Summary

- Foundations phase establishes the project foundations in terms of the business requirements, solutions development and project management
- Foundations phase should be scheduled in a fixed timebox and every effort should be made to complete it on time
- Business foundations consists of the business vision (which sets out how the business is expected to operate after the proposed solution has been developed) and the business case (which sets out the business justification for the project)
- Prioritized requirements list defines the business requirements that the project needs to deliver, prioritized by their importance towards meeting the project objectives
- Solution foundations consists of: the business area definition (which defines how the solution will impact on the business processes), the systems architecture (which defines the technical framework for the development and operation of the solution), the development approach (which defines the development standards that will be applied) and an optional solution prototype (to demonstrate the solution)
- Management foundations describe the project objectives, the project approach (buy or build, in-house or contracted out, contingency and prioritization), project management and reporting, the key deliverables and any dependencies
- Delivery plan sets out the detailed schedule for the project with key dates, resources and contingency
- Delivery control package defines the logs, reports and documents that will be used to control the project, including the risk log, change control, periodic reports, issue log, communications log, burndown charts and dashboard
- Risk log records all the identified project risks with their criticality, mitigation or countermeasures and the person responsible for implementing them
- Change control is the process that will be implemented to handle any requested changes to the high-level project scope

# 9 Development

*The development process begins with the exploration of the requirements and early prototypes in order to evolve a viable preliminary solution. This is then engineered into a fully robust operational system.*

# Development Process

Having established the firm foundations and business case for the project during the foundations phase, development work can begin. In place of the traditional project work breakdown structure, agile projects use a feature breakdown structure as illustrated in the following diagram:

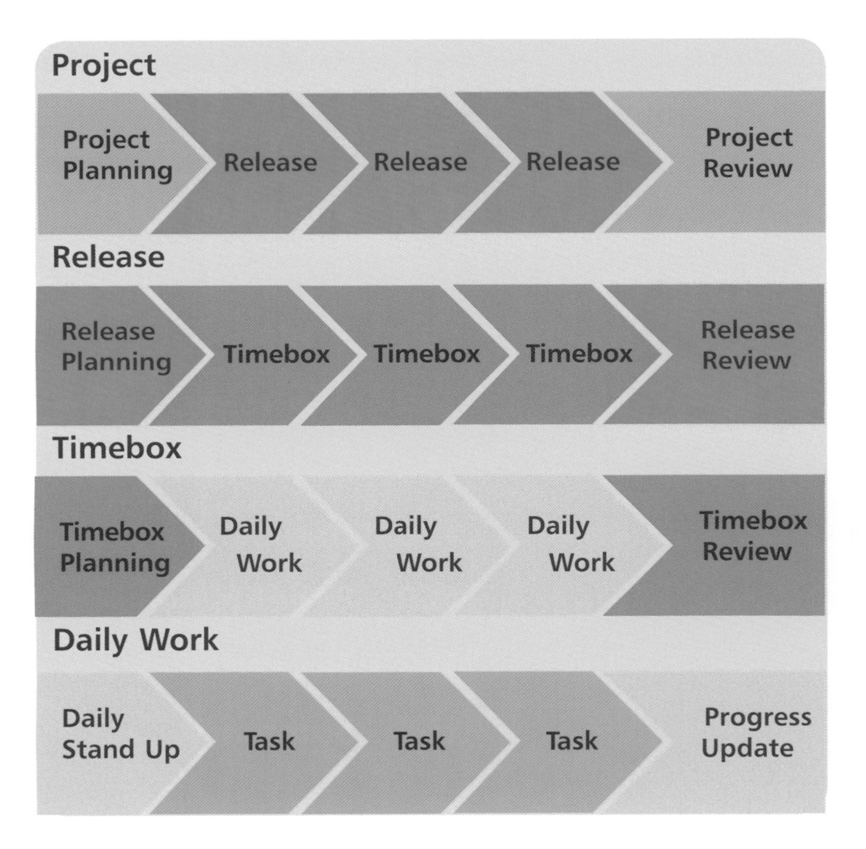


The project is broken down into the planned releases. Each release is broken down into a number of timeboxes. Each timebox is broken down into days and each day a number of tasks are allocated to members of the development team. The tasks are to develop and test the features required to satisfy the business requirements.

Regardless of the particular methodology (or methodologies) being used, the above breakdown structure accurately reflects the working method. In Scrum the timebox is referred to as the sprint while in XP and Lean Development it is the iteration.

Most of the methodologies just refer to development, while in DSDM development is split into two phases: exploration and engineering. Due to the iterative and incremental nature of the agile approach, these do not normally happen once only and not necessarily sequentially. The following diagram is extracted from the DSDM project lifecycle diagram:

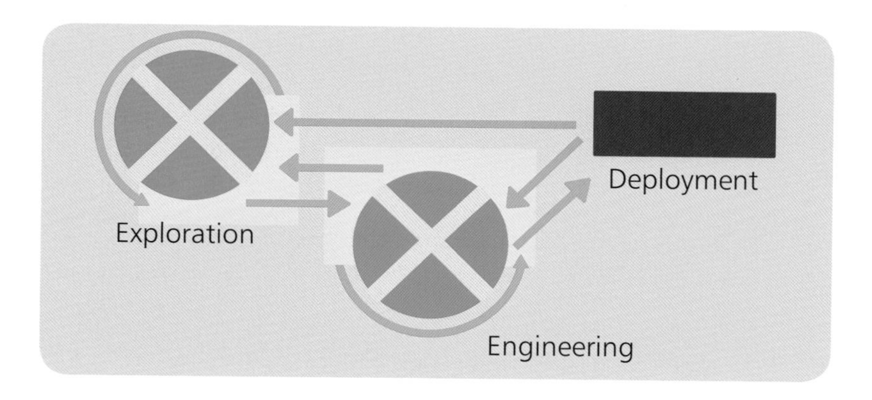


Except for small and short duration projects, the development work is normally divided up into several releases. These releases are in turn divided up into development timeboxes. There are basically three options for these timeboxes:

- Exploration timebox will be used where all the exploration activities for the increment are to be completed before engineering of the increment solution begins
- Engineering timebox will be used where all the exploration activities have been completed for the increment and the robust solution ready for deployment is to be engineered
- Combined timebox may be used on very small or simple projects where the solution developers are confident that they can explore the requirements and build the solution in a single timebox

There are multiple actual paths the project can take through these development timeboxes as illustrated above. For a large or multi-team project there may be parallel exploration and engineering phases, where one team is carrying out the exploration while one or more other teams are carrying out the engineering. The other (non-DSDM) methodologies do not make any distinction.

# Exploration Phase

The exploration phase continues to explore the business requirements and begins to develop them into a preliminary solution. This is not expected to be a ready to install solution but just to demonstrate that a suitable business solution to the requirements can be delivered.

## Preconditions

For exploration to begin there are three preconditions that should be satisfied:

- The business, solution and management foundations products have been accepted by all the key stakeholders as a suitable foundation on which the business solution can be developed
- The physical, technical and any other requirements are in place and adequate to support the development work
- All of the required development and business personnel are in place and ready to work on the project

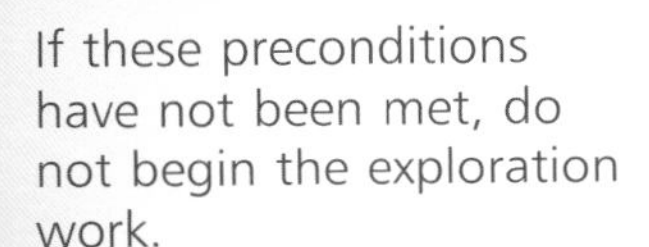

If these preconditions have not been met, do not begin the exploration work.

## Objectives

There are five objectives for the exploration phase:

1. To further develop and elaborate on the requirements established in the foundations phase as documented in the prioritized requirements log
2. To explore the needs of the business in more depth and develop more detailed requirements based on these needs
3. To build a functional and demonstrable solution that satisfies these business requirements
4. To demonstrate this early solution to the people in the business who will use, support and maintain it once it has been implemented
5. To develop further the business area and system architecture definitions produced in the foundations phase and create models that illustrate how the solution will work and how it supports the existing or planned business processes and systems

The evolving solution is covered later in the chapter.

# Engineering Phase

The engineering phase takes the preliminary solution that was created in the exploration phase and continues to evolve this iteratively and incrementally. By the end of the engineering phase the solution should have been fully tested, achieved full operational readiness and be ready to install.

## Preconditions

For engineering to begin there are three preconditions that should be satisfied:

- The evolving solution from the exploration phase has been accepted by all the key stakeholders and the business visionary has confirmed that the features demonstrated are in line with the vision for the final solution
- The physical, technical and any other requirements are in place and adequate to support the completion of the development work
- All of the required development and business personnel are in place and ready to work on the project

## Objectives

There are four main objectives for the engineering phase:

1. To further refine the evolving solution produced by the exploration phase towards a deployable product
2. To ensure that the product is compliant with any non-functional requirements
3. To test the solution against the technical and business test plans in order to meet the agreed acceptance criteria
4. To expand and refine any products or documentation that will be required to operate or support the solution in the business

Broadly speaking the exploration timeboxes are intended to demonstrate the required functionality of the product while the engineering timeboxes refine the product into a robust, business ready solution suitable for deployment.

# Timebox Plan

The timebox plan is developed from the delivery plan (produced in the foundations phase) and expands on the relevant objectives for the development timebox in question. It lists the deliverables to be produced, the activities required to produce them and the resources required to carry out the necessary work.

## Composition

The timebox plan should contain the following details:

1. Summary of the objectives for the development timebox
2. Definition of the deliverables to be produced from the development timebox
3. Key milestones such as technical and business reviews with their scheduled dates
4. Agreed MoSCoW prioritization of the products and activities within the development timebox
5. Complete list of all the resources (both human and other resources) that are required for the successful completion of the development timebox

The timebox plan should be produced by the development team leader with the involvement of the development team. It should be approved by the project manager and technical co-ordinator.

## Quality Criteria

The plan should satisfy the following quality criteria:

- Were the work effort estimates produced by the people doing the work and are they reasonable?
- Have the acceptance criteria for all the products been agreed?
- Are the identified resources available for the required time?
- Are the team certain that the Must Haves can be produced?
- Have the lessons learned from previous timeboxes been applied?

# Testing

Testing is a key element of software development projects or projects that include a software element. Testing should be in line with the test packs produced in the exploration phase. The principles of agile testing are as follows:

## Fail Fast

The sooner a defect is found the less it will cost to fix. The aim is to fail fast by testing as early as possible. This means not waiting for the product to be complete before testing it.

## Collaborative Testing

Ideally the development team will be dedicated to the project and include business, developers and testers co-located. Even if they are not, testing should fully involve the business representatives.

## Repeatable Tests

As tests will usually need to be run several times they need to be repeatable. Test management and test automation tools are widely available and will speed up the testing process significantly.

## Independent Testing

All products should be tested by someone other than their creator. This will have the advantage of making sure the understanding of a requirement is tested rather than just the code. Active involvement of business representatives in the testing can ensure that this happens.

## Prioritized Tests

In the same way that requirements need to be prioritized so do tests as it may not prove possible to carry out all the tests to products to be delivered within a development timebox. Each test should be related to a requirement with a MoSCoW priority so the test should inherit that priority.

## Test Driven Development

Tests should be specified before a product is created. This will mean that the acceptance criteria are confirmed before any potentially wasted work is spent on the wrong product.

## Risk Based Testing

Requirements should be assessed for the probability and impact of failure. Then resources can be prioritized to test the areas with the highest risk first.

Hot tip 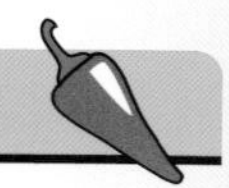

Business and technical testing and test plans are covered in the next topic: Assurance Pack.

# Assurance Pack

The solution assurance pack consists of three components that define how the constituent parts of the evolving solution will be judged as being complete and fit for purpose:

- Solution Review Record
- Business Test Pack
- Technical Test Pack

The business and technical test packs are primarily aimed at software components of the evolving solution but may also be used for the test, trial and acceptance of any other deliverable.

## Solution Review Record

The solution review record should provide a record (either formal or informal) of all reviews of components of the evolving solution. It will be used as part of the timebox review. It may not be kept in some circumstances if the business ambassador is embedded with the development team and the timeboxes are very short. Where produced it should contain a record of all:

- Product reviews carried out
- Decisions made about how the requirements are being addressed in the evolving solution
- Previously unidentified risks, dependencies or anything else that could impact on future development work

## Business Test Pack

The business test pack is developed from the business test strategy (produced in the foundations phase). It will continue to evolve as the solution evolves and demonstrate how the business testing activities are being controlled. It should contain the:

- Business acceptance test plans that show: how business testing will be integrated throughout the project; the type of tests that will be performed and their focus; who will be responsible for carrying them out; and the planned timeframe in which different levels of testing will be performed
- Business test scenarios (user stories) will define the tests that will be used to simulate the use of the evolving solution (or parts of it) in the target business environment

- Business test data will provide business information in an appropriate format that can be used for testing purposes. This could be real business information extracted from existing business processes or data created to simulate the way in which people would interact with the new business processes. It should also cover the state of the data at intermediate stages and at the end of the process
- Business test records which will be a record of the results of business testing with details of any discrepancies between the expected and actual results achieved

## Technical Test Pack

The technical test pack is developed from the technical test strategy (produced in the foundations phase) and evolves in line with the evolving solution. Its purpose is to demonstrate how the technical testing activities will be controlled. It should consist of:

- Technical acceptance test plans which will show how technical testing is being integrated into the project, the type and focus of the tests to be carried out, who will be responsible for the tests and the timeframe in which different levels of testing will be carried out
- Technical test scenarios which will define the technical scenarios that will be used to test the evolving solution (or part of it) in the target business environment
- Technical test data will provide the necessary information (data) in an appropriate format to allow the test scenarios to be performed. It may be produced from existing business information or created to simulate the way that people will interact with the solution. It should cover what the state of the data will be at intermediate stages and at the end of the process. It should also provide for testing all boundary conditions (at, above and below the boundary) where a range of values are expected
- Technical test records will be a record of the results of all formal technical testing, together with the results of the testing and details of any discrepancies between the expected results and actual results achieved.



Hot tip

Discrepancies should be documented in a way that helps those who will need to rectify them.

# Evolving Solution

The solution foundations were established in the foundations phase and consisted of one or more of the business area, system architecture and development approach definitions together with the solution prototype. This forms the starting point for the evolving solution, which will be further evolved during the exploration and engineering phases of development. As the solution is evolved into a product that can be deployed it becomes the deployable solution.

## Purpose

The evolving solution effectively demonstrates the current understanding of the business requirements. It provides tangible evidence of what progress has been made towards a deliverable solution. It also gives stakeholders outside the immediate project team an opportunity to give feedback on the current state of the proposed solution.

The evolving solution is produced by the solution development team with contributions from the business advisors and any other specialists required. Where they are relevant or add value to the evolving solution it should contain each of the following components:

## Business Model

The business model is developed from the prioritized requirements list and the business area definition (if created). It is evolved during the exploration phase and analyzes details of the requirements and the products that will be developed to address them as part of the overall solution. It is developed alongside the prioritized requirements list, which is in turn updated to reflect the analysis of requirements in the business model. The business model should:

- Expand on the detail of the requirements in the PRL
- Describe business processes that will be changed or introduced by the solution
- Analyze any dependencies between the requirements
- Identify products the development team will produce
- Sequence the products based on business priority and technical feasibility

## Design Model

The design model is developed from the system architecture definition (if created), the prioritized requirements list and business model (if created). The design model should cover the following areas:

- How the parts of the solution which impact on systems architecture should be developed
- The basis of the technical acceptance criteria for the deployable solution or relevant parts of it.

## Prototypes

As the solution is being evolved the development team will often reach a point where there may be alternative ways of dealing with specific requirements. There may also be different technical ways of meeting requirements. In these circumstances building prototypes that illustrate the alternatives can often be the best way forward. These prototypes may be discarded or become part of the evolving solution. They should:

- Demonstrate any options on the preferred way of evolving the detail of the solution
- Explore techniques or technical capabilities being considered

## User Documentation

As the solution is evolving towards a deployable solution, user documentation will usually be required. This will support the business users by telling them how to use the deployed solution in the most effective way.

## Support Documentation

The support documentation provides the technical guidance that will be required by the people who will be supporting the production use of the deployed solution. It should be appropriate for the audience and also include guidance on problem diagnosis.

## Deployable Solution

Once the evolving solution is ready for deployment, having passed all the technical and business acceptance tests it should be baselined as fit for deployment. This is regardless of whether it is actually to be deployed or not and constitutes a product deliverable that will be used in progress tracking and reporting.

# Deployment Plan

The deployment plan sets out the detailed plan and scheduled timelines for the deployment phase. It will be more like a traditional project plan in that it details the tasks to be performed and by whom, rather than the deliverables to be produced by the whole development team. It cannot be timeboxed as the scope is not variable and therefore time and resources need to be flexible.

## Composition

The deployment plan details the manner in which the evolving solution will be deployed and become operational. It also schedules all deployment activities that need to be carried out. For the reasons stated above, the deployment plan can be produced as a traditional Gantt chart although not necessarily. However it is structured it should contain details of:

1. A complete list of the work activities (tasks) that need to be completed
2. The scheduled dates for each task to start and finish, together with any milestone dates
3. The resources (individuals or groups of people) allocated to each task
4. The amount of contingency in the schedule relating to time, cost (resources) or scope

## Technical Tasks

These should include details of how the production environment (hardware, system software, security, networking, etc.) will be installed and commissioned. They should also define how the deployed software will be installed into the production environment.

## Business Tasks

These should include details of how any new or changed business processes will be implemented. They should also cover how any new or revised organizational structures will be communicated and implemented. Finally they should define how any necessary training will be carried out for the people impacted by the business changes.

Hot tip

Plan the end user training for just before the solution deployment and communicate it to the end users.

The deployment plan should be created during the exploration phase, updated if necessary and finalized during the engineering phase. It should be produced by the project manager in consultation with the team leader and all impacted parties.

## Quality Criteria

Once produced the deployment plan should satisfy the following quality criteria:

1. Has the plan been agreed with those responsible for the business use of the solution and those responsible for the technical support of the operational solution?
2. Are the cost and resource work effort estimates realistic for achieving a successful deployment of the solution?
3. Are the necessary resources available and committed to carrying out the work necessary to achieve the plan?
4. Has the proposed timetable been agreed with the business and does it meet its needs?
5. If applicable, are the procedures for handing over to support and maintenance documented and agreed?
6. If applicable, are the procedures for data loading, parallel running and system cut over documented and agreed?
7. Is the training strategy and plan adequate and appropriate for the business users?
8. Have any changes to the physical environment been identified and agreed with those impacted?
9. Have any issues relating to third parties been identified and resolved?
10. Has internal and external communication been considered and planned?



Hot tip

A template for a deployment plan is provided for your use on our website. Go to www.ineasysteps.com/resource-centre/downloads

# Benefits Realization Plan

In order to establish whether the project was successful or not it is necessary to compare the actual benefits achieved with the expected benefits, as documented in the business case. The benefits realization plan sets out how and when the benefits actually achieved by the deployed solution will be measured and compared to the expected benefits.

It should describe how the benefits will start to accrue once the solution has been deployed. It should describe the activities that will need to be carried out to measure these benefits and those responsible for them. Finally it should set out how to perform the assessment and who is responsible for it.

## Content

The suggested contents of the plan are as follows:

- A description of the information to be used
- How the baseline will be established
- How to establish that the new working practices have been properly embedded
- How the measurements will be taken
- How the results will be reported

These items are all expanded in the following sections:

## Information to be Used

Based on the expected benefits as set out in the business case, the plan should identify the information that can be measured and where it will be obtained from. It should identify when the information can be gathered in terms of the planned solution increments. Finally it should quantify the expected value for each measure of the information at various points in time.

## Establishing the Baseline

Having defined the information to be gathered, the next step is to set a baseline to establish the current values for each measure of the information. The plan should define how and when the information for this baseline will be established and recorded. It should identify who will be responsible for gathering and recording it, how it should be documented and to whom it should be reported.

The baseline must be established before the first solution deployment.

### New Work Procedures

Any new working practices and procedures need time to settle in and the people using them need to become familiar with them. There is therefore little point in measuring the benefits achieved at day one. The usual practice is to allow something like three to six months (or it could be longer for more significant changes) for the new working practices to become established.

The plan should therefore set out a schedule of the activities required to establish that the new procedures have been successfully embedded. It should identify who is responsible for carrying them out and to whom the results should be reported.

### Measurement

The plan should then describe how and when the actual measurements should be taken and who is responsible for taking them. It should specify how and by whom these measurements will then be compared to the target metrics to identify whether or not the expected benefits are being achieved. Finally how the results should be documented and to whom they should be reported.

### Benefits Assessment

The plan should then set out how and when the benefits assessment should take place and who is responsible for carrying it out (bearing in mind that this will usually be after the project has finished). Finally the plan should specify how the benefits assessment should be documented and to whom, in addition to the project sponsor, it should be distributed.

### Quality Criteria

- Does the plan include all the quantitative benefits identified in the business case?
- Is the timescale for the benefit achievement in line with the business case?
- Have the identified individuals and their management agreed to carry out the activities?
- Will the information be accessible to those responsible for measuring it?
- Is it clear who will coordinate this work?

# Timebox Review

As defined in Timeboxing (on pages 56-57), each timebox will conclude with a close out or timebox review meeting. This meeting covers a number of aims:

### Product Approval

The primary aim of this meeting is to obtain and record the formal acceptance by the business of all the products delivered by the timebox.

### Incomplete Work

The secondary aim is to make decisions about what should be done with any work that was planned for the timebox but could not be completed within it. There are basically three options:

- Consider the work for inclusion in the next timebox
- Schedule it for some future timebox or release
- Drop the requirement from the project completely

Just allowing incomplete work to roll forward into the next timebox automatically will have a snowball effect as the project progresses and the backlog builds up. If this happens then sooner or later the project timescales will be overrun.

### Lessons Learned

The final aim of the review is to look back at the timebox and review the project management, development and technical methods used and what actually happened in practice. The idea is to identify anything that can be learned to make future timeboxes more effective.

All of this information needs to be documented so that it can be considered later in the release and project reviews. Without it the project will be reliant on people's memories of what happened some time in the past. The document in which it is recorded is the timebox review record.

### Timebox Review Record

Timebox review records are produced following each review in a development timebox. They document what has been achieved, what has not been achieved, what should be done about any incomplete work together with any information that might have an impact on future plans.

The record may be very formal or completely informal according to the organization and the requirements of the project but it should always be documented in some physical form.

## Contents

The suggested composition of the record is as follows:

- Details of how successful the delivery was against the timebox plan with a list of what was delivered and what was not
- A formal record of the acceptance by the relevant business representative of the completed deliverables
- For any work not completed details of the priority of the requirement and if and when it will be completed
- Details of any lower priority requirements that are being removed from scope
- An assessment of how effective the iterative development techniques used were and how effectively the timebox control processes were
- Details of any risks, issues or other observations that were identified during the timebox
- Details of any lessons learned from the timebox and actions that are to be taken in planning future timeboxes

The review record should be produced by the development team leader with input from the development team and any other involved stakeholders. It should be accepted by the project manager and approved by the business visionary. The prioritized requirements list should also be updated to reflect any changes.

## Quality Criteria

The following quality criteria should be considered for the timebox review record:

- Does the timebox review record accurately reflect the outcome and explain any variance from the plan?
- Have the deliverables been formally accepted?
- Have appropriate actions been taken with regard to risks, issues and lessons learned?

**Hot tip**

A template for a timebox review is provided for your use on our website. Go to www.ineasysteps.com/resource-centre/downloads

# Summary

- Agile projects are broken down into releases, timeboxes, days and tasks. Although these may be called something different in other methodologies they refer to the same things
- In DSDM the development work is split into two phases: exploration (which explores the business requirements and develops a preliminary solution) and engineering (which turns this into a robust, ready to install product)
- Each timebox will have a timebox plan which will include a summary of the objectives for the timebox, a definition of the deliverables, key milestones, prioritization of the products and activities together with a list of the people who will do the work in the timebox
- Testing will be required for any projects involving software development and should aim to find defects as early as possible. It should be: collaborative, repeatable, independent, prioritized, test driven and risk based
- The solution assurance pack will consist of a solution review record, technical test pack and business test pack. It defines what will be tested and how
- The preliminary solution is the beginning of the evolving solution and will consist of some or all of: the business model, design model, prototypes, user documentation and support documentation. It will end up as a fully deployable solution
- The deployment plan is a detailed plan for how the solution will be deployed, covering the work that has to be done, the dates when it needs to be done and the people who will actually do it
- The benefits realization plan defines how the actual benefits will be measured and compared to the expected benefits from the business case, after the solution has been deployed
- The timebox review record will document the results of each review in the timebox listing how successful it was, any work not completed, details of requirements moved out of scope, how effective the techniques were and any risks, issues and lessons learned

# 10 Deployment

*This chapter covers the implementation of the developed solution and project closure following the final release.*

# Implementation

The main purpose of deployment is to implement an interim or final release of the product. Any necessary training will need to be carried out and the business will change over to using the new product, system or process. The change over should leave the end users confident and ready to use and exploit the new product.

Implementation should also cover an initial period of support for the new product (typically from one to three months). This may be provided by the project team or by a user support group if one exists in the business.

## Deliverables

The main deliverables from the implementation process will be trained end users, completion of parallel running (if applicable) and the cut over to live use of the new product.

The product should be formally handed over to and accepted by the business at the end of the cut over process. Following the final release of the product the project team can be disbanded and the project closed down.

Typical deliverables include:

- User Training
- Completion of Parallel Running
- Cut over and/or Ramp up of Production
- Business Acceptance
- Release Review
- Benefits Enablement Summary
- End Project Report (following the final release)

## Tasks

Typical tasks that will be carried out during implementation are as follows:

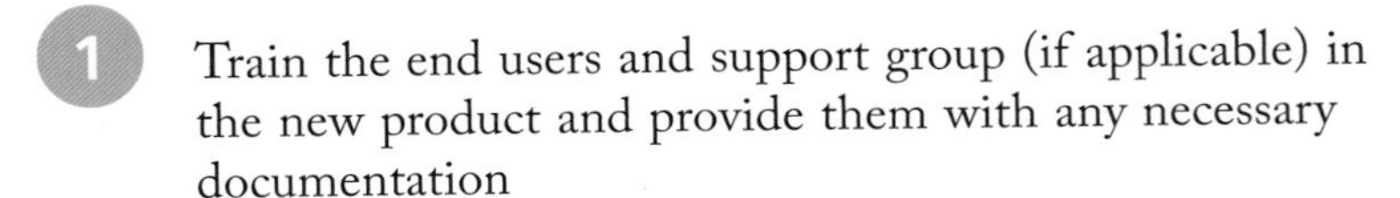

1. Train the end users and support group (if applicable) in the new product and provide them with any necessary documentation

2. Installation of production systems and any other supporting procedures
3. Carry out any preliminary data take-on or data conversion to enable the new product to function
4. Prepare for and perform cut over from the old processes to the new product
5. Support the users and operation of the new product during the critical early use period
6. Review progress of the project against plan, review and update the risks and business case and revise the project plan as necessary

Following the final product release and once things are running smoothly:

7. Complete the hand over of the product to the business
8. Plan and initiate the close down of the project
9. Prepare the End Project Report and review it with the project sponsor

Planning for implementation should have taken place during the development stage of the project, so the main effort during implementation is to make sure the users are properly trained and that the cut over goes smoothly. Problems and issues will occur and need to be addressed by the project team.

The end users will need a lot of support during the first few weeks of any new system or process so it is a good time to walk the floor and see how they are doing.

In the next topic we will examine the deployment phase and the DSDM approach to implementation.

**Hot tip**

Stay close to and support the end users as they are the key to the success of the project.

# Deployment Phase

Once a deployable solution has completed acceptance testing and been approved as fit for purpose by the business it can be brought into productive use. In DSDM this is referred to as the deployment phase. With the iterative and incremental development process, not every deployable solution is necessarily implemented and, with the amount of work involved in deployment, it is up to the business to decide if there will be sufficient benefits from implementing a new release.

Deployment of the solution may be internally within the business or, if the product is to be sold, the process is to prepare a shippable product. The deployment phase also provides a key review point prior to implementation or product release and the next development cycle.

## Objectives

The objectives of the deployment phase are as follows:

1. To implement a release of the solution into the live business environment
2. To provide any necessary training, documentation and support to the business end users of the solution
3. To provide any necessary training and documentation to the operations and support staff who will be responsible for ongoing support and technical maintenance of the implemented solution
4. To assess whether or not the deployed solution will enable the projected business benefits to be achieved
5. To review the performance of the project to date, confirm the ongoing business viability and re-plan the remainder of the project

These objectives will apply to each interim release of the product and in addition, following the final deployment of the product:

6. To close the project formally

7. To review overall project performance from a technical, development and project management perspective

8. To review overall project performance from the business perspective

### Precondition

The deployable solution must have been approved for deployment by the project sponsor and the business manager responsible for the ongoing operation and support of the solution.

### Deployed Solution

Each deployed solution is one release of a deployable solution produced by the solution development team. Once deployed it is implemented and in operation in the live business environment.

The deployed solution may be an interim solution that only provides part of the business requirements or it may be the full solution. It should allow at least part if not all the objectives of the project to be achieved. It should also allow at least part if not all of the business benefits to start to accrue.

### Quality Criteria

It should satisfy the following quality criteria:

- Do the constituent components of the solution work effectively and are they mutually consistent?
- Does the deployed solution appear to operate as expected in the business environment?

### Continuing Development

Part of the process of reviewing project performance and the ongoing development of the solution for each increment is to decide if the project should continue. The Pareto Principle states that around 80% of the benefits should flow from around 20% of the work. So as each increment is developed the return on the remaining work effort required becomes less and less.

Re-prioritizing the remaining requirements and considering the likely work effort required to produce them (based on experience to date) should enable the business to make this critical decision.

Hot tip

If the deployed solution is fit for purpose is there any real benefit in further development?

# Project Review

The project review is an on-going process that is conducted at the end of each product increment (release). The project review report is developed and evolved during the project and it consists of three component documents:

- Increment Review Record
- Benefits Enablement Summary
- End Project Assessment

## Increment Review Record

The increment review record is based on information from the timebox review records and it documents what was achieved in the creation of the deployable solution. It is used as the basis for planning further product increments, further projects and the support and maintenance of the deployed solution.

The content of the increment review record is similar to the timebox review records on which it is based. The suggested composition is as follows:

1. Details of the success (outcome) of the increment measured against the delivery plan and recording what was actually delivered and what was not
2. An analysis of the decisions made (as recorded in the timebox review records) and how they affected the way the requirements were developed
3. A record of the formal acceptance of the deployable solution by the business visionary
4. Details of any risks, issues and lessons learned from the increment

In addition where any further increments are planned it should also cover:

5. A re-assessment of the priority of the work remaining to be completed and any lower priority requirements that are to be removed from scope

6. A review of the effectiveness of the project management and development processes and techniques used in the project

And where this was the final increment of the product:

7. An assessment of the priority of any work not completed together with a plan for if and when any important requirements will be completed as part of the current project or as part of some future project

## Quality Criteria

The increment review record should satisfy the following quality criteria:

- Does the increment review record reflect the outcome of the increment accurately?
- Is there a clear explanation for any differences between what was planned and what was actually delivered?
- Have all the deliverables been formally accepted by the business visionary or have the reasons for any rejections been clearly explained?
- Have any plans for further work been accepted by those responsible for taking action on them?
- Have appropriate actions been taken to address any lessons learned in future plans?

## Production and Approval

The increment review record should be produced by the project manager with full input from the development team leader, business analyst, business visionary and any other interested stakeholders.

The review record should then be approved by the business project sponsor. This approval also signifies their recognition of the ongoing viability of the project.

The benefits enablement summary and end project assessment are covered in the following two topics.

# Benefits Enablement

The benefits enablement summary provides a link between the product that has been delivered in the increment and the business case that justified the project. It should contain a list of the benefits as described in the business case which should now start to accrue through the use of the deployed solution.

## Purpose

To document the fitness for purpose of the deployed solution by describing the benefits that should now start to accrue to the business through the proper use of the solution.

## Content

It should contain a summary list of the following:

- Business benefits from the business case that have now been fully enabled in the solution
- Business benefits from the business case that have been partially enabled in the current increment with an indication of the proportion of the benefit that has been enabled
- Business benefits from the business case that have not yet been enabled in the current increment

## Quality Criteria

The benefits enablement summary should satisfy the following quality criteria:

- Does the benefits enablement summary list all of the business benefits identified in the business case?
- Is the reason for the proportion of benefits that should accrue from the partially enabled features clearly explained?
- Are the business stakeholders in full agreement with this assessment of the deployed solution?

## Production and Approval

The benefits enablement summary should be produced by the project manager in consultation with the business analyst, business ambassador and development team leader. It should be approved by the business visionary and business project sponsor. This approval acknowledges that the solution as delivered will allow the benefits listed to accrue to the business through the proper use of the solution.

# End Project Assessment

The end project assessment is the final component of the project review report. It is created at the end of the project to summarize the success of the project.

Hot tip

This is the document on which the project manager's performance will be judged.

## Content

The following are the suggested contents:

- A summary of the success of the project in terms of what it has delivered and what it has not delivered together with any outstanding issues or actions that still need to be addressed
- The overall cost of the project compared to the original estimate produced in the foundations phase for the features actually delivered
- A record of the formal acceptance by the business project sponsor of the final deployed solution
- The process that will be followed to shut the project down once this end project assessment has been accepted
- A summary of the key lessons learned regarding the project management and development processes and techniques used

## Quality Criteria

The assessment should satisfy the following quality criteria:

- Does the assessment reflect the performance of the project in terms of what has been delivered and the cost?
- Does it explain any differences between the actual and estimated figures for work effort and other costs?
- Has the business project sponsor formally accepted the solution as deployed, if not are the reasons clear?
- Is the shut down process clear?
- Have the lessons learned been communicated for the benefit of the organization?

## Production and Approval

The end project assessment should be produced by the project manager in consultation with all other relevant stakeholders. It should be approved by the business project sponsor so that the project can be formally closed down.

Hot tip

A template for a end project assessment is provided for your use on our website. Go to www.ineasysteps.com/resource-centre/downloads

# Project Closure

The process to be followed in closing down the project should be developed and documented as part of the end project assessment. It should be agreed by the project team and approved by the business project sponsor. This topic identifies some of the areas the project closure may need to cover.

## Project Deliverables

All the major and minor deliverables from the project should have been identified and their production tracked (preferably using a configuration management system or procedure). Formal confirmation that they have been produced to the required quality, and have been accepted by the business, should all be documented. But it is not unusual to find that some minor project deliverables have been left incomplete. Checking and confirming all deliverables will ensure they have all been completed and signed-off.



## Support Arrangements

The required support arrangements for the business should all have been identified as part of the requirements. These support and maintenance arrangements should now have been set up to operate for the life of the product. The arrangements should operate fully within the business and not require any form of ongoing support from members of the project team (unless the person concerned is moving into a new role to provide it).

It is good practice to document lessons learned throughout the project. That way you won't have to struggle to remember them all at the end of the project.

## Lessons Learned

There will normally be a lot of lessons learned during the course of a project. From the business point of view, it is essential that these lessons are not lost. While the project manager might well remember and benefit from them in future, it is also important that the whole business does too. Therefore, any lessons learned during the project (however painful) should have been recorded, consolidated and passed on to the appropriate person or group within the business for onward communication. This forms a good basis for an organization's developing maturity in project management.

## Benefit Assessment

The benefits realization plan should have been produced during the development process and benefits realization should start to occur once the new product has settled in. Benefits measurement should have begun following deployment. It is usual for any new system, product or way of working to take some time before the full benefits are achieved so a date, at some specific time in the future, should have been agreed when the benefits assessment will take place.

### Close the Cost Center

Any budget authorizations or cost centers set up for the project should be closed (or frozen) so that no further costs can be charged to the project. This means the final cost of the project, as reported in the project review, will not change.

### Early Project Closure

If, for whatever reason, the project is terminated before completion, it should still be formally closed. In addition, the reasons for the early closure should be documented together with the agreed way of dealing with the situation remaining.

### Closure Deliverables

Most of the project closure deliverables should have been produced at the end of deployment. These include the project review, benefits enablement summary and end project assessment.

### Closure Tasks

The typical tasks that will need to be carried out to close the project down include:

1. Completion, sign-off and archiving of all documentation and files and hand over of project accommodation
2. Business acceptance should have been obtained for the product and it should be formally handed over to the business operation group
3. Technical acceptance for the ongoing support should have been obtained and all technical material, source code, development and test environments should be handed over to the support group
4. Confirm that benefits measurement and assessment tasks have been accepted and planned



Hot tip

Schedule a final 'thank you' celebration for the project team and invite the project sponsor.

# Summary

- Deployment covers the implementation of an increment (release) of the product with the necessary training and support of the business users
- The deployable solution must have completed acceptance testing and been approved as fit for purpose by the business
- Deployment may be within the business for an internal solution or to prepare a shippable product if it is to be sold
- The objectives of the deployment stage are to: review the performance of the project and its on-going viability; implement the solution; provide any necessary training and documentation; and to assess to what extent the solution will enable the business benefits to be achieved
- Part of the process of reviewing the project is to determine whether the project should continue or whether sufficient benefits have been achieved to make further development unnecessary
- The project review report consists of three parts: the increment review record; the benefits enablement summary; and the end project assessment
- The increment review record sets out the details of the success of the project measured against the delivery plan and records what was delivered and what was not
- The benefits enablement summary provides a link between the delivered product and the benefits listed in the business case. It lists the benefits that have been fully enabled in the product; the benefits that are partially enabled in the product; and the benefits that have not yet been enabled
- The end project assessment follows the final delivery of the product and summarizes the success of the project in terms of what was delivered and what was not; what the cost of the project was compared to the original estimate; how the project will be shut down; and the key lessons learned
- Once the end project assessment has been approved the project can be closed down in line with the shut down procedure set out in the end project assessment

# 11 Post Project

*This final chapter covers post project activities together with some tips for running a successful agile project.*

# Project Closure

Project closure should have taken place at the end of the deployment of the final release and is covered in detail in the previous chapter. However it is worth summarizing the situation that should now be in place post project.

## People

The project team, including the project manager, should have been disbanded. This means that there is no one to take responsibility for making sure things happen other then the project sponsor and the business management that have agreed to the necessary post project activities.

## Business Case

The outline business case was originally created in the feasibility phase and developed into the full business case in the foundations phase. This quantifies the expected cost of the project and the expected benefits of the project. It is the benchmark against which the actual costs and benefits need to compared.

## Prioritized Requirements List

The prioritized requirements list was originally created in the foundations phase and subsequently updated through exploration, engineering and deployment phases. It lists all of the identified requirements for the project.

## Benefits Realization Plan

The benefits realization plan was originally created in the exploration phase of development and used and updated during the engineering and deployment phases. It describes how the benefits will accrue once the solution has been deployed.

## Benefits Enablement Summary

The benefits enablement summary was created during the deployment phase. It sets out what benefits from the business case could now start to accrue if the solution is used properly.

## Project Review Report

As a part of the project review report, the end of project assessment will have been created at the end of the deployment phase. It will record which requirements were delivered and which were not against the prioritized requirements list and the cost of delivering these requirements against the expected cost of the project.

# Post Project

The purpose of the post project phase is to measure the benefits actually achieved as a result of the project and to compare these to the expected benefits as stated in the business case. The assessment should begin as soon as the deployed solution has settled down and accurate measurements can be taken. This will normally be between six and twelve months after the completion of the project.

## Objectives

The only objective of the post project phase is to assess whether the benefits described in the business case have actually been achieved through the business use of the deployed solution.

## Preconditions

The solution should have been successfully deployed, settled in and become 'business as usual'. That is to say the business users will have become fluent and fully competent in using the solution.

## Measurement

In order to allow the benefits assessment to take place the necessary data must be gathered and recorded in an appropriate form. This will have been defined in the benefits realization plan. The benefits realization plan will have set out the following:

- What information can be measured after the solution has been deployed
- When these measurements should be taken
- Where the information required for the measurements is to be obtained
- How the information is to be gathered
- Who is responsible for providing the information, measuring it and reporting it to the business project sponsor and other interested stakeholders

## Baseline

The benefits realization plan should also have set out how, when and by whom the pre-deployment measurements should be captured. This forms the baseline against which the post project measurements can be compared to identify the actual benefits achieved. It should have taken place early in deployment.

Always take the baseline measurement before the first release is deployed.

# Benefits Assessment

It is not unusual for businesses to avoid production of the final benefits assessment. Not enough time or too many other things to do are the frequently quoted excuses. The real reason will often be concerns about whether or not the actual benefits justify the project. However, failure to do so misses a key opportunity for a business to understand the quality of and opportunity to improve its business decision making process.

## Benefits Assessment

Once all the necessary measurements have been taken the benefits assessment can take place. This should describe how the benefits have actually accrued following the deployment and production use of the solution. Where the benefits are not all expected to accrue in the same timeframe it may be necessary for the benefits assessment to be repeated a number of times with cumulative results until the final assessment can be made.

## Contents

The suggested composition of the benefits assessment report is as follows:

- Brief management summary of the results of the assessment and the overall success of the project
- Quantitative descriptions of the actual benefits that the deployed solution has achieved
- Analysis of any differences between the actual benefits and the expected benefits forecast in the business case
- Details of the actual measurements and baseline measurements used in the assessment

## Management Summary

The management summary should bring together the final results of the project, listing the expected cost and benefit and the actual cost and benefit. It should simply state whether or not the project was a good business decision.

## Expected Benefits

The report should itemize all of the benefits identified in the business case with an indication of whether they were fully implemented, partially implemented or not implemented.

### Actual Benefits

Against each of the expected benefits the report should list the actual benefit achieved, with the before and after measurement.

### Differences

The difference between each expected benefit and the actual benefit achieved should be listed, followed by an analysis of the reasons for the difference and any follow on actions that might be appropriate.

### Unexpected Benefits

While they should not form part of the formal assessment, it is a good idea to record any other unexpected or unforeseen benefits. These often occur as an indirect effect of a project and as they were not forecast they may be difficult to quantify. They can be things such as improved cash flow, reduced carbon footprint and better customer satisfaction.

### Appendix

Details of the actual measurements, the processes used and any other relevant information is probably best put in an appendix to the report for any interested parties.

### Quality Criteria

The benefits assessment report should satisfy the following quality criteria:

- Does the benefits assessment cover all of the benefits expected at the start of the project and as described in the business case?
- Are the achieved benefits clearly attributable to the use of the deployed solution or is it possible that other factors could have resulted in the figures?
- Have any variances been satisfactorily explained as far as it is possible to do so?

### Production & Acceptance

The benefits assessment should be performed by the business visionary with input from the business stakeholders. It should be accepted by the business project sponsor who will distribute or publish it in line with business practice.

The Benefits Assessment measures the success of the Business Case not the Project which is measured in the End Project Assessment.

# Project Success

Don't forget

The benefits assessment measures the success of the business case, not the project.

Success for the agile project manager is measured by whether the project is on time, within budget and with all the 'must have' requirements implemented. This topic lists 20 tips for a successful agile project:

1. In agile projects the cost and time are fixed and the features are variable so concentrate on keeping the project on time and within budget
2. The agile project manager is a facilitator and motivator, not a task master, so manage with a light touch and keep the team happy
3. Plan the project from the strategic level down to the timeboxes and allow the development team to organize themselves and plan the detailed work
4. The essence of agile projects is that the requirements will change so forget change control and welcome the features backlog/prioritized requirements list
5. Track and monitor progress at the strategic level using feature burndown charts and timeboxes and share this information with the development team
6. Full business or customer involvement is crucial for the success of an agile project, not just by the project sponsor and business management but also the real end users
7. Use the Pareto Principle: 20% of the effort will deliver 80% of the benefits so use this to appraise the plan for each timebox and release
8. All agile methods are good and complimentary, so embrace whichever agile methods the development team and organization want to use
9. DSDM gives an excellent framework for managing a project using agile project management

10. Scrum is a first rate methodology for the development team to use in managing and optimizing the development process
11. Extreme Programming builds on the other agile methods and delivers good results quickly
12. Lean Development focuses on eliminating waste, making decisions as late as possible, delivering fast, empowering the team, building in integrity and keeping a focus on the big picture
13. Develop a communications plan for the project including the daily stand-up, feature burndown charts, project dashboard and management reports
14. Don't strive for perfection (gold plating), in an agile project fit for purpose is good enough
15. Deliver on time, every time and make sure the whole team are committed to this goal
16. Use facilitated workshops for effective brain-storming, information gathering and decision making
17. Prioritize requirements, bug fixes, changes and testing with the business using the MoSCoW rules
18. Use models and prototypes to illustrate potential solutions as early as possible in the project
19. Estimates should always be produced by the people who will do the work and reinforced with feedback on their actual project velocity
20. Don't produce anything that doesn't add value to the project but see the next topic for some key deliverables

**Hot tip**

There is an old saying that there are no good project managers only lucky ones. So think agile and stay lucky!

# Key Deliverables

Agile principles dictate that nothing should be produced that does not add value to the customer. The following key deliverables have been proven to help the agile project manager stay in control of the project and therefore add value:

1. Terms of Reference: the objectives of the project and the business reasons for carrying it out. While this is considered an optional deliverable by many, the lack of it will mean the project has no clear direction

2. Business Case: the justification for carrying out the project rather than doing something else with the money and resources. Again this is considered an optional deliverable by some but its absence indicates a lack of commitment by the business

3. Feasibility Assessment: to document the results of the feasibility study showing that the project is viable from a business and technical perspective. The lack of this could result in a lot of wasted work before realizing that the project is not viable

4. Models and Prototypes: throw-away examples of the proposed solution or parts of it to enable the business and other stakeholders to get an early view of the solution. The sooner people start to see the solution the sooner they can confirm that it is going in the right direction

5. Project, Release and Timebox Plan: to give a strategic (high level) overview of the whole project. This gives the project team and all other stakeholders a clear picture of the project

6. Prioritized Requirements List (Features Backlog): to list the features that the project is required to deliver with an indication of how critical they are to the business

7. Test Plans: plan how products will be tested as fit for purpose before starting to develop them

8. Deployment Plan: to show how the solution will be deployed and what activities will be needed to ensure it is used successfully

9. Burndown Charts: give a visual indicator of progress against plan that the team and all other stakeholders can easily understand

10. Benefits Realization Plan: to demonstrate that the project is delivering the required solution and identify how and when the business benefits can be measured

11. Timebox Review: every timebox should end with a review or close out meeting to formalize the acceptance of the solution by the business, make decisions about what to do with any incomplete work and capture any lessons to be learned for the future

12. User Training Plan: plan and schedule any required end user training well in advance and make sure it is communicated to the end users

13. Delivered Solution: the most important deliverable of all and the reason for the project. The interim releases provide tangible evidence of the work and progress of the project and the final delivered solution marks the completion of the project

14. Project Review: to assess the success of the project against the plan: were the increments delivered on time and to budget? What was delivered and what was not? Can the benefits now be assessed? This is what the project manager will finally be judged on

15. Benefits Assessment: to provide the answer to the ultimate question: was it worth it? This compares the final outcome of the project back to the business case. What benefits did the project really deliver?

**Don't forget**

Project Reviews and Benefits Assessments will help to improve future projects.

# Summary

- Starting a project the right way is critical but so too is closing it down. It is a chance to make sure that everything has been completed and accepted by the business
- The post project phase is mainly concerned with measuring the actual benefits that the delivered solution is providing to the business
- The benefits realization plan should have determined what information will be needed, where it will come from and who is responsible for gathering it
- The baseline for the existing (pre-project) situation must be measured before the first release of the new solution is implemented so that the 'before' figures are available
- The benefits assessment should list all of the expected benefits together with the actual benefits achieved with an explanation of any variances
- There will often be additional unexpected or unidentified benefits and it is worth recording these as well
- While the benefits assessment measures the success of the business case, it should not be used to judge the success of the project or the project manager
- Project success and the success of the project manager is judged by whether the project was completed on time, to budget and with the 'must have' requirements met
- Make sure the business end users are fully involved in the project to deliver a product that will meet their needs
- Use the Pareto Principle (80/20 rule) to judge whether it is worth developing the next timebox or release
- Don't strive for perfection (gold plating) when 'fit for purpose' is all the business needs and it will always deliver better value for money
- While nothing should be produced that does not add value to the project there are a number of key deliverables that should be produced

# Index



## A



## B



## C



## D

## E

## M



## N



## O



## P

## Q



## R



## S

## T



## U

## W